Living with Change

Ursula Markham is a practising hypnotherapist, counsellor and business training provider. In addition to running her own successful clinic, she gives lectures and conducts workshops and seminars in Britain and abroad. She has appeared frequently on radio and television and is Principal of the Hypnothink Foundation, which is responsible for the training of hypnotherapists and counsellors to professional level.

Selected titles by the same author:

The Beginner's Guide To Self-Hypnosis

Bereavement (Vega Guides Series)

Creating A Positive Self-Image

Ultimate Stress Handbook For Women

Women Under Pressure

Contents

To Philip and David
– with all my love

Every person, all the events of your life are there because you have drawn them there. What you choose to do with them is up to you.

Richard Bach, *Illusions*

1

The Certainty of Change

THE DIFFERENT TYPES OF CHANGE

The one thing we can all be sure we have to face in life is change – however it may arise. There are those changes which leap upon us unexpectedly and for which we may be totally unprepared, while others are the result of long and careful planning on our part. There are inevitable and progressive changes and there are changes which creep up on us so slowly and surreptitiously that we may not even be aware that they have occurred until some time later. But every change, however it happens, is bound to have an effect upon us and our future.

Because no one lives an entirely isolated existence, the way we react to those changes which occur will affect not only ourselves but all those who come into regular contact with us. Our attitudes to other people, to events – even to life itself – may alter dramatically because of the changes with which we are faced. It is as well, therefore, to look at the various types of change which may arise, to be as well prepared for them as possible and to see that our futures are enhanced rather than diminished by the results.

Change can come in many forms and may be welcomed or feared. Perhaps we should first consider the different types of change:

1

Deliberate change

This can be anything from the minor (a new hairstyle, changing the route to work) to the eventful (moving house, a new relationship, giving up your job) and the effects upon you will naturally vary according to its importance. But at least you will have had the chance to prepare for the deliberate change, to plan it over as long a period as you wish and to anticipate its outcome. Even if the final result is not as you had originally intended, you will discover as you read further that careful anticipation of various possibilities can help to prevent a great deal of the stress or trauma normally associated with change.

Involuntary change

The man or woman who is involved in a plane crash, who is suddenly made redundant or whose lover deserts them for another – these are some of the victims of negative involuntary change. Positive involuntary change may involve winning the football pools or meeting the man or woman of your dreams, either of which occurrences sounds delightful and yet the effect on the individual can be just as traumatic as can the effect of negative change. Here, of course, there has been no opportunity to prepare oneself for the alteration in lifestyle which will necessarily result and so the shock to the system can be even greater.

Progressive change

There are some changes which are inevitable. We are all going to grow older; we are all going to have to cope with the loss of someone for whom we care deeply; we are all going to die ourselves. We realize these facts from the moment we are old enough to understand what happens in life. All the fighting and the protestations in the world cannot change it but none of these events needs to be viewed negatively. Each can be seen as part of some other greater pattern of which we will hopefully gain more awareness as time goes on.

Short-term change

There are, of course, some changes which are comparatively short-term and after which things will return to their previous position. Or will they? Even if you think that, after a brief stay in hospital, a fierce argument with your partner or a visit from great aunt Maud, the previous status quo will be resumed, you are wrong. No change occurs in life which does not bring in its wake some difference in the people it has touched. Perhaps the stay in hospital awakens in you fears about your health which previously never existed. The argument may make you see your partner through different eyes, and great aunt Maud may tell you something about your relatives which will cause you to look differently at another member of the family in the future. In their own way, short-term changes can have as dramatic an effect on you as those which are intended to be permament.

Long-term change

Whether deliberate, involuntary or progressive, the long-term change is seen as a complete alteration in oneself or one's way of life. Somehow the very inevitability of the new position often seems to make it easier to accept. As you will discover, there is nothing more stressful than fearful anticipation of change. Once it has happened and there is nothing you can do about it, it is amazing how quickly most people are able to come to terms with any new situation. But 'coming to terms' does not mean blind, passive acceptance. It has far more to do with learning to face the new position with positivity and treating it as an exciting challenge which brings its own special rewards.

CHANGE AND YOUR HEALTH

Change – good or bad – arouses many different emotions. It can be the source of excitement, fear, guilt, joy, anger or grief. If the changes which occur are not to cause undue pressure on you, it is vital that you learn to recognize and release these emotions. Attempting to stifle your true feelings can not only cause physical and mental problems in the future but can also send the wrong message to those around you so that they fail to understand what you are experiencing and are therefore unable to be helpful or supportive.

All change is traumatic and stressful – even when it involves the happiest of occasions. You have only to think of the panic in the household of any bride in the run-up to the wedding to realize that, even when anticipating a joyous event, those most closely involved in it are put under great pressure.

In 1973 T. H. Holmes and R. H. Rahe developed the Life Change Index so that the possibility of health change in people could be measured. They discovered that, by looking at the number and type of changes which had occurred during the previous twelve months, it was possible to predict the chance of any individual experiencing a major change in his or her health. This Index takes no account of education, intelligence, sex, race or class, or the fact that some people are basically stronger than others and better able to cope.

The Index itself consists of a list of events which could happen to anyone's life within a given year. Each event is given a numerical score. The higher the total score of any individual, the more likely he or she is to suffer some stress-related illness (mental or physical). To discover your own rating, study the Index and place a tick by all those events which have happened in your life during the past year.

LIFE CHANGE INDEX

Event	*Score*
Death of spouse	100
Divorce	73
Marital separation	65

Now add up your total score. If this comes to 150 or more, you have a fifty per cent chance of undergoing a health change. If your score is 300 or more, you have a ninety per cent chance of undergoing a change in health.

Those results are based upon work with people who have done nothing to prepare themselves for the effects of change upon their lives. By reading this book and putting into effect any of those techniques which you feel are applicable to you, you can greatly reduce the likelihood of any major health problems arising as a result of the changes you encounter.

It is interesting to note that Holmes and Rahe did not specify that changes had to be for the worse to be stressful. You will note that they list such things as 'change in financial state' and 'change in living conditions'. They do not say that your financial state has to deteriorate or that you have to move from a palace to a hovel for the change to be stressful. Indeed, you may remember that some years ago a lady who won a fortune on the football pools announced delightedly that she was going to 'spend, spend, spend'. A few years later she was penniless and alone. The increase in her financial position had done little to bring her long-term happiness and had resulted in a great deal of stress.

LEARNING FROM CHANGE

Change of any sort – whether it appears at first to be positive or negative – should be treated as part of life's learning process. It can help us to develop and to evolve both on a practical and on a spiritual level – and this applies whatever your particular religious or spiritual beliefs. Life itself is a learning process and everything that happens within it adds to that process. The degree of learning and development will naturally depend upon each of us and our willingness and ability to see the significance of the changes that occur and to incorporate them into our lives in the most positive way possible.

If all this sounds a little like a Pollyanna-attitude,

whereby the response to anything which happens is to count your blessings, let's look at a particular case history to see how a positive attitude to a negative change enabled one woman to improve her life.

When the woman (I'll call her Ellen) first came to see me, she was in a most distressed state. Unable to suppress her tears she explained to me that, after thirty years of what she had considered a happy marriage, her husband had announced that he was leaving her to go and live with a younger woman with whom he had fallen in love. Ellen was distraught. She felt abandoned, ashamed and humiliated and was worried about what her friends would say. She felt she could not cope with sympathy and dreaded the fact that they might side with her husband and desert her.

Financially Ellen would not be too badly off. Her husband was prepared to make her a reasonable allowance but the house they had shared for twenty years – the home she loved – would have to be sold and the money divided between them. Her children were caring and supportive but they were now adults with families of their own and did not live near their mother. And, as she told me, she did not want to become a burden on them either emotionally or financially.

Ellen did not know how she was going to cope. Her husband had always earned good money and she had not worked outside the home since her children were born. Never having been involved in it, she knew nothing about the practical side of dealing with bank accounts and household expenses. She blushed as she confessed 'I don't even know how to change a plug – I'm so useless.'

There was nothing to be done about the situation between Ellen and her husband. He was now living with the woman he intended to marry as soon as the divorce was made absolute. So we had to begin with that knowledge and start from the present position, looking towards the future.

The first thing we did was to itemize the problems Ellen was facing. It is amazingly helpful to see things written down in black and white. Difficulties do not seem as enormous on paper as they do when they are chasing each other around inside your head. And, of course, as you deal with each one in turn, there is both relief and a sense of achievement in being able to cross them firmly off the list.

In Ellen's case making a list also helped to deal with the insomnia which had arisen since her husband had told her of the situation. She felt that she had so many problems to face and so many worries to deal with that she could not relax her mind sufficiently to sleep. And when utter exhaustion finally brought sleep to her, that sleep was unsettled and fitful as her anxieties invaded her dreams. Listing her problems on a sheet of paper seemed to Ellen rather like putting them away for the night. They would still be there the next day but, there being nothing at all she could do about them at two in the morning, she was able to set them temporarily aside and to get the sleep she so desperately needed. I did suggest, however, that she kept a pen and pad on her bedside table so that, should a new problem present itself in the middle of the night, she could write it down immediately and, knowing she could now forget it, go back to sleep.

Ellen's list read as follows

1. *Money*. How will I manage? Will I have enough? How do I deal with banks, building societies and so on?
2. *Household tasks*. What do I do if something goes wrong in the house?
3. *Moving home*. Where will I go? Can I afford it? Who will help me?
4. *Friends and family*. How will I tell them? How will I face them?
5. *Loneliness*. How will I cope?

I asked Ellen how she felt when she looked at her list. She told me that, although it covered major issues and she was still frightened at the thought of having to take charge of her life, seeing the words in black and white did help to reduce the terror of the situation. I reminded her that, in addition to crossing out any item on the list when she felt she had dealt with it, she could add to it too. If a sudden fear entered her head, rather than let it cause her pain and anxiety, she should write it on her list as another item to face.

Of course, there was nothing to say that she had to face each problem alone. Whether she sought help from her friends, her children, official bodies or a professional consultant, she should never feel that she was completely isolated. And although to each of us it usually seems that we are the only person in the world facing a particular set of difficulties, logic tells us that this is just not true. There is no problem in the world which has not been faced by someone in the past and will not be faced by someone in the future. This statement is not intended to minimize the way you feel but to reassure you that there are methods already in existence for helping you cope.

And there is no shame in asking for help. Advice centres and professional helpers exist for that very purpose. And real friends will be only too pleased to play their part. After all, if someone you considered a friend approached you and asked for your help, would you turn your back on that person or think any less of them? Of course not. You would be pleased to offer assistance if you could. Pay your own friends the compliment of allowing them to do the same for you.

To begin with, Ellen and I sat and quietly discussed the items on her list and how she thought she might deal with them. Here are some of the ideas we came up with:

1. *Money:* Here Ellen was luckier than many women who find themselves in her position. Her husband was not a poor man and – perhaps due to feelings of guilt – he had already told her that he was prepared to settle a reasonable sum on her. In addition, there would be her share of the sale of the house. She would not be rich but she would have enough to cope adequately. We sat down and worked out some figures and Ellen was able to see that she would have enough to buy either a flat or a smaller house and to pay her expenses. Had she not been in this position, she would have been able to seek advice from the relevant departments who would have told her about ways of bringing her income up to a reasonable level.

As for the unfamiliarity with the procedures of banks and building societies, Ellen decided to make appointments with the appropriate advisors in those establishments to ask for help in the day-to-day management of her financial affairs.

2. *Household tasks:* Ellen was worried that she would not know what to do if something should go wrong in the house – perhaps a fault in the plumbing or electricity. Naturally no one can say that such a situation will not arise at some time in the future so I asked Ellen what would give her peace of mind in the present. She said that she would feel better if she knew who to call on for help so we decided that it would be a good idea – *now*, while nothing was wrong – to compile a list of nearby plumbers, electricians, repairers and so on and to keep it near the telephone. Then, if a crisis should occur, she would immediately know to whom she could turn. As for minor problems, such as changing a plug, she only had to follow the accompanying instructions.

3. *Moving:* When dealing with the first item on her list, Ellen had already worked out how much she would be able to afford to pay for a new home. Rather more difficult was the decision as to whether she should leave the area altogether – perhaps to go and live nearer to one of her children – or to stay in a place she was familiar with and where she already had friends. This was a decision only she could make; no one can really advise in this situation. Ellen decided to stay in the same town so that she could keep in contact with her friends. She felt that, much as she loved her children, she did not want to become too dependent upon them as might happen if they were the only people she knew in her new district. And, of course, there was nothing to guarantee that *they* might not want to move in the future and she did not wish either to be left alone knowing few other people or to cause them to feel uncomfortable about making the move because of her.

As for the practicalities of looking for a new home, once again Ellen could consult the professionals and her solicitor would take care of the legal aspect for her.

4. Friends and family: Ellen had, of course explained the situation to her two married children and they, not unexpectedly, had been both caring and supportive. But she felt far more awkward about telling more distant members of the family and her friends – particularly those who had been friends of both her and her husband. I told her that I felt it extremely unlikely that there was anyone who did not already have personal knowledge of a divorce or separation among their acquaintances. Distressing as it is for the people concerned – and whether you consider it a good or bad thing – divorce is a fact of life as we approach the end of the twentieth century. People are no longer shocked by it in the way that they used to be. Anyone who is a friend will neither judge nor criticize; anyone who does sit in judgement is not a friend in the first place and really should not matter.

One thing I did urge Ellen to do was to tell her friends as soon as possible. I have learned from working with people that they tend to become resentful if they 'discover' that someone about whom they care has been going through a personal trauma and has not trusted them sufficiently to tell them about it and to allow them to give emotional support.

Because telling other people was something that was causing Ellen real distress, we spent some time talking about it and how she would cope with it. She felt that, if she were to telephone a friend to explain the situation, she would become tongue-tied and embarrassed. So I suggested that she might care to sit down and prepare a script setting out what she wanted to say in the way she wanted to say it – giving as much or as little information as she wished. She would not have to read word for word from this script but she could keep it by her when she made the telephone calls and it would be there for her to glance at whenever she felt lost for words.

Scripting is a useful tool whenever you want to pass on information to someone else. It gives you a chance to set your thoughts in order before you make the call or write the letter. And, although it will always be there for you to refer to, it is often the case that the reassurance brought about by its existence is enough to make it unnecessary when the occasion actually arises.

5. *Dealing with loneliness:* This was Ellen's greatest fear of all. She was afraid that she would spend the rest of her life sitting alone in her home with no one to talk to or to go on holiday with. And, of course, there is no denying that suddenly finding yourself alone after spending all your adult life as part of a partnership can be a daunting prospect. It wasn't that Ellen was wondering whether or not she would ever marry again – the trauma of the separation and divorce caused her to be too emotionally numb to even worry about such a possibility. She was concerned about all the days and evenings which would comprise her future.

The problem was eased a little because Ellen had already made up her mind that she would not move away from the district in which she had lived for so long. So she would still have the same friends she had always had and there was no reason why those friendships should come to an end.

She wondered whether she should look for a job. But, at the age of fifty-two, not having worked for so long and taking into account the current employment situation, it seemed unlikely that she would find one. In addition, any money she earned would be deducted from the amount her husband was paying her so she would not even be any better off financially. We discussed the possibility of her becoming involved in one of the voluntary organizations who are always in need of helpers. This would give her a sense of purpose, a way of occupying her time while bringing benefit to others and also a means of meeting a whole new group of people.

Or she could consider attending day or evening classes in any subject which interested her. This too would give her mental stimulation and would bring her into contact with other people who presumably would share at least one of her interests.

As for holidays, if she did not feel that she would be happy to go away with one of her friends, she could perhaps go on a special interest holiday. It is not at all unusual to find single people of all ages taking part in such vacations and, once again, there would be the bond of a common interest to break the ice when meeting other participants.

Once we had discussed all the different problems on her list, Ellen felt that she had a blueprint from which to work. No one could pretend that the change in her life which had been forced upon her was easy to deal with or that she was happy with the situation. But the change was inevitable and the only thing she could do was to find a way of coping with it in the best way she could. There would still be days when she would feel lost and alone – but they would grow fewer and further apart. She could choose how she looked upon the whole situation; it could be an ending or a beginning. I am pleased to say that Ellen decided to look upon it as a beginning and the last time I heard from her (some two years after the divorce) she was managing extremely well.

If you ever find yourself faced with a change which causes you to feel fear or anxiety about the future, take a leaf out of Ellen's book and start making that list. When you see your problems written down in front of you, you have a starting point from which to work. And *doing* something – however small that something may be – brings a sense of achievement and reduces the worry as you realize that you have control over your own life. Use the charts below as a starting point:

What is causing me anxiety? ....

....

What aspects can I do nothing about? ....

....

What are the benefits, however trivial, of the current situation? ....

....

What are my greatest fears?

1 ....

2 ....

3 ....

4 ......ๅ...

What can I do about each?

1 ....

2 ....

3 ....

4 ....

Having dealt with the most immediate problems, it can be helpful to think about the more distant future. Naturally none of us can be certain about what will happen in years to come, but in many cases it is possible to have a fairly good idea of the direction one is going to take. Think about the positive future aspects of your current situation; what is there that you can look forward to? If you find negative thoughts insinuating their way into your mind, don't try to *force* them out as you will merely succeed in causing yourself a great deal of stress. Look at those possible negative future aspects and ask yourself how you would deal with them should they arise. Hopefully you will never have to put these plans into action but it can be extremely reassuring to know that they exist.

Another thing you can do when faced with a stressful situation brought about by an unwanted change in your life is to draw up a balance sheet indicating both the positive and negative long-term aspects of this change. One word of advice – don't try and do this all on one day. If it happens to be a day when you are feeling strong and in control, you will have lots of positive aspects and very few negative. Whereas, if this is a bad day, I can imagine how long your negative list would be! Try compiling your balance sheet over several days and you are more likely to get a realistic summary of the situation.

Look on each change in your life – however it comes about – as a new and exciting challenge. The world would be an extremely boring place if nothing ever changed. Just look at nature itself; observe the changes in the seasons and the positive and negative aspects of each. And yet, even taking those negatives into account, would we really wish them to be different? If we did not have the snow in winter, would the daffodils of spring be so vibrantly beautiful? Isn't there a magnificence in the hues of autumn, even though the falling leaves tell us that colder times are approaching? Every change has a plus side and a minus side and you have the ability and the right to choose which one you are going to concentrate on.

None of this means that you have to meekly accept each and every change with which you are faced. There may be some which are reversible if you will only make the effort to fight them. There are others which can be modified or the inevitability of their consequences avoided. Of course in such cases you must do what you feel is right to deal with the situation. But, should you be faced with an in-evitable change in your life, then there is no point in kicking and railing against it. The only result will be to increase your own stress and distress. In such cases, acceptance is necessary in order that you can then go on to control your own future as much as possible.

As you read this book, you will find ideas, techniques and methods for dealing with many types of change in a positive way, helping you, I hope, to enhance your own growth and development.

2

Letting Go

To deal positively with changes which occur in your life and to allow yourself to benefit from them, you need to allow yourself to become as flexible as possible. It is the supple tree which bends in the gale while the one which is stiff and rigid either snaps or is pulled up by the roots. In the same way, the more you are able to develop a flexible attitude to life and its changes, the more you will not only survive those changes but actually come to see them as another step in your own personal evolvement.

One of the essentials if you are to become more flexible in your outlook is to develop the ability to let go. Letting go does not merely imply that you are able to put past events behind you but that you are able to discard old ideas about yourself as well as those you hold about other people.

The world is full of people who are only too happy to put others into pigeon-holes, not simply because of colour, religion or nationality, but also because of the way they dress, the way they speak, the part of town they live in and any number of other reasons. We all know that the majority of football fans are genuine supporters and not hooligans, that not every retired colonel is a closet racist and that the majority of teenagers are living reasonable and trouble-free lives. The problem is that it is so simple to categorize people – and this problem is often made all the greater by the less responsible sections of the media.

When did you last see a banner headline proclaiming 'Teenager is kind to elderly neighbour'? That isn't news. So, because we tend to hear only about the wrong-doers and trouble-makers, it is easy to forget that they are in the minority. It is rather like aeroplane flights; we never hear about all those which reach their destination safely – only the few which crash.

This habit of putting people into pigeon-holes arises largely because of outside influence. It may be due to the media, it may be due to repeated statements by people who are bigoted in outlook – but if something is repeated often enough it is all too easy to assimilate. One of my patients who had been told by her husband over a long period that she was 'stupid' said to me: 'I know I may not be the cleverest person around but I also know that I am *not* stupid. And yet, when you hear that claim day in and day out for ten years, you actually begin to believe it.'

If we can have the wrong idea about other people because of influences upon us, we are even more likely to have the wrong view of ourselves. Like it or not, we have all been 'programmed' by the views, statements and attitudes of other people since our earliest childhood and the impression of ourselves with which we grow up is often created by past people, situations and events. If we are to learn to let go of the past, any misconceptions formed in this way must be abandoned too. Every individual, once old enough to understand the effects of the past on their current image of themselves, has the right and the ability to work on their self-image and to change it.

UNDERSTANDING YOUR SELF-IMAGE

Before you can change, however, you need to know what you are like now. It is easy to think that we know and understand ourselves, yet quite a simple test will show us that we certainly do not see ourselves in the same way that others now do. So who is right and who is wrong – and why are there these often conflicting views? Try the following experiment and see whether you encounter any surprises.

1. *What do I think I am like?* (List those characteristics which
you feel apply to you):

Positive traits   Negative traits

_____   _____

_____   _____

_____   _____

_____   _____

2. *How do I believe other people see me?*

Positive traits   Negative traits

_____   _____

_____   _____

_____   _____

_____   _____

_____   _____

3. *How do other people tell me they see me?* (Here you will
have to enlist the help of a good friend or someone who
can be trusted to tell you the truth):

Positive traits   Negative traits

_____   _____

_____   _____

_____   _____

_____   _____

I wonder how many surprises turned up in answers to
No. 3. Many people are quite astonished to discover how
others perceive them. Among my own patients I have had
a young woman who felt that she was completely lacking
in personality ('wishy-washy' was how she described herself) while others considered her charming and gentle; a

man who told me that he was relatively confident and self-assured and who was extremely hurt to discover that colleagues – and even his wife – felt that he was pushy and self-opinionated; and a teenage girl consumed with shyness whose friends had originally thought her to be stuck-up and stand-offish.

Take some time to look through the answers, both your own and other people's. Compare them and see if you can come to an assessment of your own personality which is as near reality as possible. Now you have something to work upon; you will have begun to know yourself – an essential if you are to be able to let go of past influences.

Those past influences will have been responsible for the view of yourself you had formed. It can be helpful to look at the people and events in the past which have combined to help you form this self-image for, if you are either to make deliberate changes in yourself or to accept external changes as they arise, you need to understand who you are and why you have become so.

If your image of yourself is a negative one, it does not necessarily mean that the people with whom you came into contact in the past were unpleasant or wished you any harm. It could be that they were weak or perhaps so over-protective and smothering that they have left you with feelings of vulnerability when compelled to stand alone.

Of course the greatest influence on your early life was your parents (or those who stood in that position). Because as little children we believe that our parents are all-knowing and all-powerful, should they reject us or be over-critical of our performance (whether in reality or simply in our own imagination) we grow up to think that we really are lacking in some way. Some people spend the rest of their lives trying to prove their worth to a father or mother, often long since dead, because this would make them, in their own eyes, a better person. Their logical mind may tell them that their parent's demands upon them were unreasonable – but the subconscious holds fast to the image impressed upon the young mind.

Similarly, should a parent disappear from the scene

while a child is still very young, that child may well feel rejected and, because in the childish mind the parent could do no wrong, may grow up to feel that he or she is unworthy of love and deserves rejection. The adult will then go on to form relationships with those whom the subconscious recognizes are bound to treat them in the same way. Every subsequent rejection serves to reinforce the negative self-image and fix it more firmly in the psyche. The tragedy is that the early rejection by an admired parent may not have been deliberate at all. Sometimes a mother or father may have to spend a long period in hospital or may even die. Fifty years ago many fathers were away for long periods of time fighting in the war. Unless such situations are handled extremely carefully, the effect upon the child can be just as traumatic as when one parent or the other deliberately deserts the family.

If you are to be able to understand yourself and your own inner image, it is beneficial to look back at the past and analyse why and how your opinions about yourself were formed. Here are some questions to help you make a start (and I am sure you can continue with others for yourself):

- What kind of people were my parents (temperament, personality, and so on)?
- Father:
- Mother:
- Which one did I prefer as a child?
- Why?
- How did I get on with brothers/sisters (if applicable)?
- Was I jealous of the attention paid them by one or both parents – and, if so, was this jealousy justified?
- How did my parents get on together?
- Were they demonstratively loving towards me and towards each other?
- Was either parent absent for a long period during my childhood?
- Did they give me encouragement and praise or were they often critical of my achievements?

CHANGING YOUR SELF-IMAGE

Once you have had time to think through these and other questions, you should be able to understand more about yourself and your past and how great an influence it has had on your present personality. Then you have a choice. You can continue through life with your present self-image – and, if you are happy with the way you are, there is no reason why you should not do so. Or you can refuse to let the past win and make deliberate efforts to change.

Changing your own inner view of yourself is not easy but, if you are less than happy with the way things are, it is certainly worthwhile. Because your self-image will have been formed at the most impressionable period of your life, and because you will have gone through the intervening years doing all you can to reinforce it, it takes a real effort to alter it. You may find that you are capable of doing this for yourself or you may prefer to seek professional help from one of the many complementary therapists who specialize in such work. As a hypnotherapist, I have helped many patients to let go of the past and create a new and more realistic self-image but that is not to say that other therapies cannot also be beneficial.

Sometimes it is helpful to go back and look at a situation which occurred in childhood but to look at it through the eyes of an adult rather than the impressionable child you used to be.

Jeanette came to see me after a series of disastrous relationships. She could not understand how, as an intelligent young woman of thirty-two, she allowed herself to be attracted time and again to the type of man who was going to treat her badly and cause her unhappiness. Her ex-husband had turned out to be an alcoholic and would, when drunk, become verbally abusive, often reducing her to tears. A former relationship had come to an abrupt end when the boyfriend, in a fit of temper, had become physically violent. And even the man whom she was currently seeing would constantly belittle her in front of others – but as yet she had done nothing to break off the relationship.

During our initial discussion, Jeanette told me that she could remember being interfered with sexually by her stepfather when she was about eight years old. However, she informed me, she had come to terms with the knowledge and had had no contact with the man since the death of her mother five years earlier. When I suggested that it might be helpful if she were regressed under hypnosis to the time of the abuse, she agreed but did not think there would be much to gain from the experience as she had already thought about it and decided to put it out of her life.

Jeanette proved to be an excellent subject and regressed easily to the age of eight. Using my detachment technique which ensures that the patient will be able to observe and report upon a situation without having to undergo either physical pain or emotional distress, I took her back to the first time her stepfather had come into her bedroom late one night. She was able to describe to me precisely what happened – and it tallied in every detail with what she had told me earlier.

I then took her on to the days following the event and asked her what had happened and what she was feeling. She said that her stepfather had told her she must say nothing to her mother because she would not be believed – it was to be 'their secret'. Not liking what was happening but feeling powerless to stop it, the young Jeanette believed that she was bad and wicked and (because adults were always right) only getting what she deserved. So, as every child in such a situation, she was not only unhappy but she suffered greatly from feelings of guilt for what was going on.

This time, however, there was a difference. Because of the detachment technique, Jeanette was now viewing the situation through the eyes of a thirty-two-year-old woman and not through the terrified eyes of an unhappy eight-year-old. This time she was able to experience anger at the man who had treated a vulnerable little girl so badly.

Sadly, many children are abused in different ways and at the time they all have certain emotions in common. They feel wicked, unhappy, frightened, guilty or ashamed.

The one thing they do not feel is anger. It takes an adult
who can look on the situation from the outside to experience rage – although this may show itself in different ways
depending upon their present personality. One will
shout, scream or swear while another will quietly and
calmly voice their new-found feelings. The way the anger
manifests itself does not matter; the two important points
are to experience it – and then to let it go. Festering hate
can do just as much damage to the personality as sub-
merged guilt.

There are those – usually people who have not received
any help with their problem – who carry their rage and
their hatred with them for the rest of their lives. But, not
only does that cause them even more suffering, it is letting
the past perpetrator win, years after the event. And they
should not be allowed to do so.

Once you have acknowledged your feelings of anger,
there are ways of expunging these understandable reactions to what was done to you in the past. Some people
find it helpful to speak aloud all the things they would like
to say to the person who hurt them – even though that
person is not present. Others will write a letter – one
which is never to be sent – expressing in whatever terms
they choose the emotions they feel and their opinion of
their tormentor. It does not matter what method you
decide to use; there are three essentials:

1. Acknowledge your true feelings;
2. Express them in whatever way you wish;
3. Having dealt with them, make a deliberate decision to
let them go. There is nothing you can do to take away the
past but you can eliminate any harmful effects it might be
having upon your present and – even more important –
your future..

In Jeanette's case, once she was able to express her feelings of anger and contempt towards her step-father and
then make a decision that she would not allow him to
destroy any more of her adult life, she found that she was
able to form new relationships based on an entirely different footing. No longer did she subconsciously see herself

as a natural victim so no longer was it necessary for her to find a partner who would treat her as if she were one.

I am not trying to pretend that, even when you know the reasons for your subconscious image of yourself, you will find it easy to change overnight. Your subconscious has created that self-image and it will seek to maintain it as change can make it feel uncomfortable. But the release and the improvement in your life can be so great that it is well worth persevering and concentrating on the 'new you'. Some people find that affirmations are helpful: for example, repeating to oneself at regular intervals phrases such as:

'I cannot change the past but I can choose not to allow it to affect my present or my future', or

'I am now free of any bad feelings about myself and can love myself as I deserve.'

If affirmations are not for you, you might try visualizing yourself in various situations acting and reacting as befits someone with a positive self-image. Perhaps you will see yourself being more assertive, either at home or at work. Perhaps you will imagine yourself having a conversation with a friend or relative, looking and sounding like someone who deserves to be treated well and refusing calmly to allow yourself to be put upon. This does not mean that you have to become aggressive, shouting at all around you. To be truly assertive you do not have to raise your voice at all. You simply have to explain quietly what your feelings are. If you feel angry, simply say 'That makes me feel angry' and tell the other person why.

If it takes time to change your own self-image, it follows naturally that it will also take time to change the way in which you are perceived by others so you may have to make allowances for them in the beginning. If they have always thought of you as having a particular personality, they are not going to be able to know, just by looking at you, that you have undergone a metamorphosis in your emotional life. This will only dawn upon them as they see the changes in your behaviour in the weeks that follow.

Although the change in your self-image will not be

immediate, we are not talking about years – or even months. The subconscious can learn to accept new information in about three weeks provided that information is constantly reiterated (hence the need for affirmations or repeated visual images). If you want to prove that to yourself, try the following test.

Select any object which you have around you every day. Let us suppose, for the sake of this example, you have chosen a waste paper basket which you keep to the left of your chair or desk. Now move that waste paper basket and place it to your right. See how long it takes for you to stop throwing rubbish on the floor to the left of you – I wager it will be less than three weeks!

You may feel that all this dwelling on the past and the effects it has had on you is a miserable thing to do but, however painful some of the memories, it does have great benefits too:

- You will grow in self-understanding. You will now be in a position where you are more able to understand why you have developed in the way that you have – both positively and negatively.
- Any person, situation or event in the past which has had an unreasonable hold on your character can be relegated to where it belongs – the past.
- By being better able to understand yourself, you will be better able to empathize with others, to listen to them and to help them where possible to overcome their own problems.
- Personal progress is not really possible without self-understanding. Unless you know why you are as you are, you cannot expect to know how to change.

In some ways you must be grateful to your past – even to the bad experiences. Without it, you would not be the person you are today. And the very fact that you have chosen to read this book means that you have a considerable amount of sensitivity and a desire to change. Had your past been all plain sailing, perhaps you would not have developed into a person with the ability to think deeply and to look beyond the superficial. So don't waste

time being sad or bitter about earlier events – just look at
them and let them go. You have no further need of them.

Any past failures on your part should be seen as positive learning steps. After all, there is no such thing as the
person who has never failed at anything (which is just as
well – think what a bore they would be!) The only thing
that matters is the way in which you regard those failures.
You can use them as a stick with which to beat yourself – 'I
am no good; I always get it wrong.' Or you can see them
as lessons – 'That way doesn't work; how else can I do it?'

Even champions in their field have failures. There is no
skater who has never fallen over on the ice, no soprano
who has never sung a wrong note and no tennis player
who has never served a double fault. But these people do
not immediately throw their hands in the air and give up.
They try and improve their performance by weighing up
what made them make the mistake in the first place and
then they put it behind them and go forwards.

Once you have learned to understand yourself better, it
is easier to progress towards the type of future you would
like for yourself. Because your self-image will be stronger
and more positive, you will be better equipped to cope
with any involuntary changes which may be thrust upon
you. You will have the confidence to deal with progressive
and inevitable change and, most important of all, you will
be in an excellent position to make positive changes for
yourself.

LIFE PLANS

Making life plans is something we tend not to be very
good at, preferring to muddle along, coping with whatever life may throw at us. But, although there will always
be circumstances which you cannot foresee, it is possible
to know the direction you would wish your life to take.
Many people who have reached the top of their chosen
professional tree will admit that they knew very early on
what they wanted to do and never doubted for a minute
that they would achieve their desires.

There is no time like the present, so why not start now and see if you can work out some life plans for yourself. Let's begin with long-term aims and ambitions – changes you would like to make in your work or home life. To do this it is necessary to be as spontaneous and trusting of your subconscious as possible. Answer the questions below as quickly as you can – don't stop to weigh up your decisions. The more instinctively you work, the more likely you are to come up with the most appropriate answers.

Long-term goals

In ten years time I would like the following statements to be true about:

My health

1. _____

2. _____

3. _____

My working life

1. _____

2. _____

3. _____

My emotional life

1. _____

2. _____

3. _____

Any other area of my life

1. _____

2. _____

3. _____

I wonder whether any of those answers surprised you. If you really worked quickly and spontaneously, I expect one or more of them did. We often smother our innermost hopes and desires, possibly thinking them too far beyond our grasp.

Medium-term goals

This next section requires a little more thought – although we are not looking for anything too detailed. Take each of the above wishes in turn and ask yourself what would be the halfway stage on the way to achieving it. For example, if you are at present working for someone else and yet under 'working life' you have put 'to run my own company', the halfway stage might be 'to become self-employed' – nothing more precise than that. Following that train of thought, fill in your answers below:

The stepping stones to achieving my aims are:

My health

1. _____

2. _____

3. _____

My working life

1. _____

2. _____

3. _____

My emotional life

1. _____

2. _____

3. _____

Any other areas of my life

1. _____

2. _____

3. _____

Short-term goals

This stage is where the real thinking comes in because this is where you need to decide what your next step is to be in each case. So this is the section which may take you the greatest amount of time to complete. Looking at each mid-term goal in turn, make up your mind how you are going to set about making it reality. Don't even begin to consider your long-term goals at this point; if you work on the immediate steps to be taken to achieve the mid-term goals, the rest will take care of itself.

Let us go back to the previous example. If your mid-term step was 'to become self-employed', there are several things you need to do. Here are just a few of them:

• Decide what type of work you wish to do. In these days of re-training opportunities you are not quite as bound by what you do already as you might think. You might choose to expand upon what you have already learned or worked at or you might wish to acquire a completely new skill. If you are really unsure about which direction you wish to go in, there are career aptitude tests available – but it is probably better to base your decision on your own instincts and ask yourself what you would really *like* to do.

• What sort of training (if any) will you require? If this applies to you, make enquiries at colleges and training agencies to find out what courses exist.

• What financial help is available? This changes from time to time but there is always something upon which you can draw. At the time of writing, you could approach such bodies as your local Enterprise Agency which will give you advice about any grants which may be available to those setting up a new business. There is also an enterprise allowance of a set amount per week for the first year of a new business venture. Many local colleges and polytechnics have units which provide free practical training during the first year of business and there are other support schemes available which vary according to the type of business and the part of the country.

- Will I need premises or can I work from my home? If the former, you will have to look into costs and suitability; if the latter, you will have to consider the legal aspect – particularly if other people are to be involved.
- What preparation can I do before leaving my present employment? If you prepare the ground as well as possible before quitting your current job, you will be better equipped to begin earning money as soon as possible.

Using the above as an example, work through your mid-term goals and see what immediate steps you can take towards achieving them.

Steps I can take now or in the immediate future to achieve my mid-term goals are:

My health

1. _____

2. _____

3. _____

My working life

1. _____

2. _____

3. _____

My emotional life

1. _____

2. _____

3. _____

Any other areas of my life

1. _____

2. _____

3. _____

You have now created for yourself a blueprint for working towards the goals you have chosen. Remember that it is not just the final goal which should be rewarding – you should enjoy yourself along the way.

Whether the changes which occur in your life are involuntary or self-instigated, it is not possible for them to be purely external. All changes either start within you or will be reflected within you – and positive change cannot be truly beneficial unless you are able to let go of the subconscious effects of previous negativity in your life.

3

Physical Change

We all realize that, from the moment we are born, we change physically day by day in appearance and in health. Sometimes these changes are for the better and sometimes they are unfortunate but, whatever they may be, it is the way we perceive them which governs how well or badly we cope with them.

APPEARANCE

It would be easy to think that changes in appearance are changes which take place on the outside alone. And yet it is impossible to separate these physical changes from our inner view of ourselves. If one person believes himself to be ugly or unprepossessing, then, no matter how good-looking he may really be, he will subconsciously give off an aura of unattractiveness. And those around him – possibly quite unknowingly – will respond to that aura rather than to his true physical appearance.

Similarly, we have all seen people, famous or otherwise, who are not particularly good-looking in the accepted sense but who have what can only be called charisma. The dictionary defines charisma as 'a personal quality or gift that enables an individual to impress and influence many of his fellows'. It is something which is possessed by those who are most successful in walks of life which put them in

32

the public eye as well as by more private individuals. It transcends the purely physical and is extremely difficult to quantify. And yet we somehow know when it is there and when it is not.

Charisma comes from within. It is more than confidence; it is an awareness of one's own value yet it does not involve conceit. It is the ability to love oneself in the true spiritual sense of the word, having nothing to do with vanity or narcissim. And it is an attractive quality which draws other people towards the one who possesses it, warming them in its glow.

Some fortunate people seem to have been born with charisma but anyone can learn to feel comfortable with themselves and to believe in their own value as a worthwhile human being. And this will reflect in their outward appearance. A belief in yourself may not give you a retroussé nose or make your feet two sizes smaller, but it can help you to develop that outer glow which transcends such unimportant details.

You can take steps to change your clothes or your hairstyle; you can diet and exercise to become slimmer and fitter; all this will be to no avail if you have not worked on your inner self too. In recent years it has become fashionable to approach a colour consultant who will advise you on which colours you should or should not wear to enhance your appearance. One of the reasons for the success of such consultants has little to do with the colours themselves and far more to do with the fact that, if you have been told that you look wonderful in red, you will remember that fact every time you put on a red outfit. Because you *believe* you look wonderful, you will feel wonderful and will give off the type of glow (or aura) which convinces other people that you do indeed look wonderful.

As a hypnotherapist I am often asked to treat patients who wish to lose weight. Some of these people may have only about half a stone to lose. To many this would not appear to be too great a problem but, if it is causing distress to the patient, then it is a problem. Similarly, if someone is two stone overweight but is not in the least worried about it, then no problem exists. Because of this, I never judge when a patient has reached the 'correct' weight by any of the printed charts and tables available. If he or she is comfortable with their appearance and the way they feel, then they have reached the right weight – whether this is two pounds more or less than the recommended figure on the chart.

An anorexic, of course, who may be so painfully thin that her very life is threatened, will still believe herself to be fat. Anorexia and bulimia nervosa are, however, deep-seated psychological problems and are not brought about simply by an over-zealous weight-loss regime. Although there are exceptions, in most cases it involves a girl in her teens or early twenties; in many cases there is a problem with the mother/daughter relationship and usually it is a signal that, for whatever reason, the girl has a subconscious wish to remain a protected child rather than face the world as a grown-up woman. Such problems should always be treated professionally, whether by orthodox medicine, complementary medicine or a combination of the two.

One of my patients, who was on the road to recovery after several years as an anorexic, used to say to me: 'I know what I weigh; my logical brain tells me that it is not enough for my height and age – but when I look in the mirror I still see this huge, fat person looking back at me.' And yet she was able to look at other people and assess correctly whether or not they were overweight. She only had this blind spot in relation to herself – another case of self-image transcending reality.

Any plastic surgeon can give you details of cases where the surgery has been successful and yet the patient has remained in the depths of depression. The real problem was not, therefore, the over-large nose or the protruding ears but the way that person saw themselves on the inside. If the physical appearance is treated without there being any counselling or analysis of the personality, there may be little or no change in the patient who had previously been attributing all his unhappiness and his lack of confidence to his outer self.

The same thing can work in reverse. Several years ago I

met a young, aspiring actress whom I shall call Marie. She was a pretty girl with a bubbly personality and was beginning to be sought after to work in both films and television. One day, during the course of a publicity photo session, the photographer asked her to turn her head a little so that 'your nose doesn't look quite so long'. From that moment onwards Marie was convinced that her nose was too long, was spoiling her appearance and thereby lessening her chances of succeeding in her chosen profession. It didn't matter that everyone else did their best to reassure her that there was nothing wrong with her nose and that it certainly made no difference to her acting ability or the likelihood of her being employed as an actress. Marie became more and more despondent until finally she decided to use every penny of her savings to have her nose professionally re-shaped by a plastic surgeon.

No one told Marie, after the operation, that the new nose – prettily shaped as it might be – seemed to detract from her appearance rather than enhance it. She was overjoyed with the way she now looked and convinced that there would now be no stopping her progress in her career. And indeed there was not. She went from strength to strength, working both in Britain and the United States, only giving up some years later when she decided to stay at home and look after her young children.

Why did Marie's personality improve so dramatically after the operation? Not because of the new nose – there really had not been anything wrong with the old one – but because of the way it made her *feel* about herself. Showing, once again, that it is the inner face which matters and not the superficial outer appearance.

How does this affect you? What can you do to improve your own inner face and thereby your own confidence? You could start by asking yourself a few questions:

• How much does my outer appearance matter to me and in what way? Perhaps you are someone who only feels content when smartly dressed and beautifully coiffed. Or maybe you are happiest in casual clothes which are

comfortable and easy to wear. Neither of these is 'right'
or 'wrong'. Spend a moment or two thinking about
which way you prefer to be dressed. Never make the
mistake of sacrificing comfort for appearance whatever
style you choose. You only have to look at the face of
someone whose shoes are too tight to see that it does
nothing for your outer appearance!

• What are my best features? (You do have some, whatever you may believe – everybody does!) What can I do
  to enhance them?
• What are my worst features? What can be done to
  change or disguise them?

You may decide to seek outside help for either of the last
two, whether from a professional or from a good friend
who will give you genuine advice.

• Do I believe myself to be an attractive person? Don't
  answer this relying purely on what your mirror tells
  you. Think about whether you have friends and how
  much those friends seem to like being around you.
• Do I have a habit of comparing myself unfavourably to
  other people? If you do, perhaps you need to go back to
  the previous chapter and ask yourself why. Was there
  something in your upbringing which programmed you
  to feel inferior? Did someone else continually compare
  you unfavourably to others? If so, perhaps it is time to
  let go and refuse to allow them to govern your present
  life.
• What does my logical brain tell me about those who are
  superficially beautiful – are they necessarily happier,
  more fulfilled or more popular? Next time you are with a
  group of people, take a look at those who are the centre
  of attention; are they really the prettiest or the most
  handsome? And what about poor, lovely Marilyn
  Monroe?
• Do I really believe that other people spend all their time
  looking at my appearance? How often it is possible to
  spend an hour with a friend and yet not be able afterwards to describe exactly what they are wearing? It isn't
  that you are unobservant or that you don't care. It is

because that person is your friend and you like being
with them that their appearance is really unimportant.
And anyone who is going to value you for your appearance alone is not worth having as a friend in the first
place!

When I was a child of about seven, a girl came to my
school who had a large strawberry birth mark covering the
whole of one cheek. At first we were all very conscious of
this – and, being small children, very curious about it.
Later, when I was about twelve, a newcomer to the school
asked me about 'the girl with the big red stain on her face'
and I really had to think hard before I knew who they
were talking about. I had known this girl for so long that I
never actually noticed the mark any more; she was just my
classmate.

HEALTH

Variations in the condition of your health naturally bring
about physical changes. These changes may be temporary
or permanent; the way you deal with them and the way
you live with their results will also determine your mental
and emotional well-being.

The holistic approach

Holism involves consideration of the person as a whole –
mind, body and spirit – and, although this chapter is
dealing predominantly with physical changes, it is impossible to separate these from your mental, emotional and
spiritual state. Each one of us consists of these four parts
and however much we may concentrate our attention on
any one of them, it is impossible to ignore the other three.
Separate bowls of flour, sugar, eggs and fat may be dull
and uninteresting but blend them together and you can
make a delicious cake. Similarly, anyone who concentrates
on any of the four personal elements (physical, emotional,

mental or spiritual) to the detriment of one or more of the other three cannot be a complete person.

One of the major differences between orthodox and complementary medicine is that the latter tends to treat the whole person while the former merely deals with a variety of symptoms. What is the point in taking pills to cure insomnia without trying to find out what is causing the sleeplessness in the first place? High blood pressure can be lowered by means of medication but surely it is important to discover its cause and work to prevent its recurrence. A complementary practitioner, whatever the therapy, is trained to help the patient discover the cause of their condition and, by dealing with that cause, to eliminate the symptoms.

Changes in health may fall into any of the three categories mentioned – deliberate, involuntary or progressive.

Deliberate change in health

A health change does not automatically refer to a deterioration. Many people spend time and energy improving their physical health and thereby their mental state. We have heard a great deal in recent years about the value of exercise; much of it seems to refer to the physical condition and, valid as this is, often ignores the mental and emotional benefits which arise. But ask anyone who follows a regular regime – whether he runs, swims, cycles or takes any other form of physical exercise – and he will tell you that not only does he find himself growing fitter and trimmer but, however tired he may be at the end of a session, he also experiences a 'high' which is lacking should circumstances cause him to miss his usual routine. (By the way, wherever I refer to 'he' or 'him', please accept it as referring to anyone – male or female. I am not being sexist but it is so clumsy to keep repeating 'him or her', 'his or hers' and so on.)

The reason for this high feeling is the surge of oxygen to the brain brought on by the physical exercise. It has been shown that, not only does the person concerned feel a sense of elation but his mind is actually sharper and he is better able to perform well in tests of mental agility soon after an exercise session. This is why it is often recommended that (provided you are used to it) you allow time to go for a run or take some other form of exercise on the morning of an important test or exam.

Another way in which people set about improving their physical condition is by learning to relax – and, even if this sounds as though it is the opposite to exercise, it is just as important. Once again, the effect is noticeable on the mental, emotional and spiritual state of the individual as well as on their physical body.

Physical effects of relaxation
• lowering of blood pressure
• reduction in heart/pulse rate
• less tension in the muscles
• reduction in adrenaline
• increase in oxygen

Emotional effects of relaxation
• reduction in stress
• less likelihood of negative emotions (anger, guilt and so on)
• increased feeling of being in control
• sensation of peace

Mental effects of relaxation
• ability to think more clearly
• increase in right-brain (creative) activity
• fewer stress-related barriers to learning
• improved memory

Spiritual effects of relaxation
• increased sense of personal awareness
• improved ability to meditate or visualize
• increase in intuitive powers
• induces a sense of harmony with others and with the world

You can see from the above that learning to relax can not only reduce the immediate stress from your daily life but can lead to an improvement in your general sense of wellness – a truly holistic approach.

You may choose to practise this relaxation with the help of a therapist (perhaps hypnotherapy, shiatsu or aroma-therapy), in a class or group (yoga or meditation) or on your own at home. If the last of these is your choice, you will find plenty of assistance as various techniques are described in books (including my own *Elements of Visual-isation* and *Your Four-Point Plan for Life*) or on specially designed cassettes. (Details of books, organizations, cassettes and so on will be found at the end of this book.)

Whatever method you decide to use, you will only have to practise relaxation for a comparatively short time to discover its benefits and the way it can enhance your life, helping you to make those changes you wish to make and to cope with those which are thrust upon you.

Involuntary change in health

Involuntary health change may occur as the result of an accident or the onset of illness and its results may be temporary or permanent. Whatever the cause and how-ever prolonged the condition, it is possible not simply to cope with the situation but actually to benefit from it.

You may be wondering how an accident or illness can bring benefits in its wake but this can occur in several different ways:

• If there is a chance that your illness has been precipi-tated by negligence in your lifestyle, its onset may make you realize that it is time to make some deliberate changes. If your physical pattern has been defective, perhaps you will decide to improve your nutrition or take more exercise. If your condition has arisen because you allowed yourself to become susceptible to stress-related illness by overdoing things or allowing yourself to be pressured by everyday events, perhaps you will set about changing your behaviour pattern and improv-ing your lifestyle in these areas.

- A period of ill-health – particularly if you have always been someone who was robust and hearty – may help to make you more tolerant and sympathetic towards those whose health is frequently under par.
- If you have suffered an accident – whether or not it was your fault – you will probably become a more caring and careful person in the future.
- Even if you have the misfortune to find that you are suffering from a condition which is said to be permanent, there may be areas of positivity:
  – You may try to learn more about complementary and self-help techniques. At best these can bring about considerable improvement but, even if this is not so in your case, you will have opened your mind to concepts and techniques which may previously have been unfamiliar to you and such awareness is always of benefit even if at first we do not understand how this is to be.
  – The human mind, body and spirit are wonderful at compensating for a breakdown in any area. We have all heard of examples of blind men and women whose hearing develops to a state of achievement far beyond that of sighted people. In recent years, thanks to the development of computer technology, it has been possible for those who formerly seemed to be trapped in their own world of non-communication to make their thoughts and feelings known. Wheelchair-bound people have been able to develop other areas of their bodies to become sportsmen and women of merit while some who have had limbs amputated have managed to find a way to overcome their disability and achieve marvellous feats of physical endurance – often in aid of charity or for the benefit of others.
  – You have only to visit a hospice to see for yourself the wonderful strength of spirit and peace of mind many of the patients are able to achieve with the help of the people who care for them. It is difficult for those of us not suffering from a terminal illness to understand this serenity but anyone with any sensitivity cannot doubt that it exists. There is an aura of spirituality which surrounds such people, who have come to terms

with their own frailty and fate. Not only does this help the patients themselves in their last months but it brings great comfort to the friends and families who love them.

Those are some of the positive results of involuntary health change – but of course, depending on your reactions and your ability to cope, results may also be negative.

– Fear of the long-term effects of your condition may slow down your recovery. It has been shown over many years that those who have a positive attitude towards themselves and their ability to heal return far more quickly to good health. Your subconscious responds so forcefully to the atmosphere around you that – whether you are in hospital or at home – care should be taken to ensure that this atmosphere is as optimistic and positive as possible. And if you can be allowed to use self-help techniques to play a part in your own cure, so much the better.

Hypnotherapists have known for a long time that the subconscious is capable of 'hearing' what is going on even when you are under anaesthetic, so it is very important that theatre staff are careful not to say anything during the course of an operation which might be detrimental to the later recovery of the patient. In recent years I have had four patients who, under hypnosis, were able to tell me of negative remarks made while they were in the operating theatre – remarks which caused each of them to suffer unnecessary doubts and fears long after their physical body had healed. Fortunately some of our teaching hospitals now appreciate the reality of this situation and strict instructions are given to all those concerned in hospital and theatre work. At least two of the major London hospitals now play cassettes of positive affirmations to anaesthetized patients during the course of an operation and it has been found (hardly surprisingly) that these patients have, in fact, made a more rapid return to full health than those who have not had the same benefit.

– Fear for the future. If you have had an accident or

suffered a breakdown in your health, whether major or minor, it is not unusual to become more cautious once you are fully recovered. Now a certain degree of caution is not necessarily a bad thing; the problem arises when undue emphasis is placed on the fear so that it overrides all other considerations. And, of course, extreme fear is an illness in itself, whether we are talking about a phobia, a panic attack or the onset of extreme stress – or any of the conditions which can have a long-term negative effect on the health of the sufferer. So, if your illness or accident has pointed out to you an area of your life where you were previously perhaps a little careless or has left you with a weakened part of your body, by all means bear this in mind once you have recovered, but do keep a sense of odds and do not allow fears and over-protectiveness to stifle your actions in the future.

– If you feel (or someone else tries to convince you) that you were in any way to blame for the accident you suffered or for a breakdown in your health, take care that a sense of guilt does not cause you ongoing distress. Certainly, if you were at fault, you could try to learn a lesson from your error but remember that having failed at something is only beneficial if we learn from that failure and make a deliberate effort to change a particular aspect of ourselves or our behaviour. Once you have learned that lesson, there is nothing to be gained – and, indeed, much harm to result – from repeated self-criticism.

– The sudden necessity for unexpected medical or hospital treatment can be traumatic in itself. Not only does it necessitate making various practical arrangements in relation to work and personal life, but it reminds us of our own vulnerability and mortality – something most people would rather keep locked firmly away in the back of their mind. There can also be the physical shock to the system of medication used or as the result of pain, and the ongoing results of such shock are all too frequently ignored. Many people, believing themselves to be fully recovered– and indeed appearing to be so – find themselves suffering a relapse or even a completely different set of problems as a result of allowing their relief at being well once more to plunge them back into an excess of activity far too soon. Because it can be just as harmful to overdo the convalescence or to allow fear to govern your behaviour, this is a point at which careful thought needs to be given to the rate at which former activities and responsibilities are taken on and it may be that outside advice or a transition period of help from a complementary therapist would be beneficial.

– The effect on other people of a breakdown in health or an accident suffered by you can also be quite traumatic. Not only do those who care for you receive a shock when they hear of it but extra stress or responsibility may be laid at their door as a result of your incapacity. Your awareness of this, however willingly they undertake any extra duties, can cause you to feel guilty or unhappy and this can impede your own progress towards full recovery. Perhaps the easiest way to come to terms with this is to involve yourself in a 'spiritual barter system'. Make yourself a promise that, once you are fit again, even if those nearest to you who are helping you now are never in a position to need similar aid from you, you will one day give such assistance to someone else who is in need of it. If everyone were to make such a commitment and stick to it, perhaps it would be possible to return to the days when people were happy to help their neighbours and there would be less need for state intervention.

Progressive ill health

There can be few more devastating moments than the one when you are told that you have a health condition which is going to become progressively worse and may perhaps even end your life. Naturally the emotions experienced at such a time will be traumatic – anger, disbelief, fear, hopelessness are to be expected and, in fact, there would be something terribly wrong if they were missing. It is how the patient reacts after running the gamut of these emotions which is important and may make a considerable difference to his physical, mental and spiritual well-being in the years to come.

There are several points to bear in mind if you (or someone you care about) have been told that you suffer from a chronic or progressive illness:

- Even if the diagnosis is correct (and presumably in such a case you will have sought a second or further opinion), treatment and knowledge are changing all the time and what is considered a permanent condition at the moment may not be so in a year or two. It was not so many years ago that Dr Christian Barnard performed the first successful heart transplant operation and it was considered wonderful that the patient survived in relatively good health for about a year. Now, even if not exactly an everyday occurrence, such operations are carried out regularly on adults and children with wonderful results, the former patients going on to live healthy and energetic lives. Research is being carried out all the time, so there is always the possibility that what seems life-threatening at the moment may soon come to be regarded differently.
- If you have a condition which at the moment is incurable, it does not follow that it is not controllable or that life cannot be enjoyable and worthwhile. From asthma to cancer, migraine to multiple sclerosis, therapies exist which can help the patient to control pain and overcome symptoms. I am not suggesting that you abandon whatever medical treatment has been prescribed but that complementary medicine can accompany it and bring great benefits to the sufferer. Most of these complementary therapies (and you will find various organizations listed in the information section at the back of this book) concentrate on the holistic approach, that is, working on the whole person (including the emotional and spiritual) rather than dealing with individual symptoms.

One of my own patients, whom I'll call Eric, has multiple sclerosis. When he first came to see me he was suffering from a number of symptoms. These included blurred vision and a numbness down one side of his body while the other side was so hyper-sensitive that, if a droplet of water splashed on to his skin, it felt as though he had been burned. Eric still has multiple sclerosis but, by working on his emotional and spiritual self in conjunction with the physical, his symptoms have receded and he has returned to work.

- It may be that you are going to have to give up, or change, some of the things in life which have previously given you pleasure. Whether it is the diabetic who can no longer enjoy certain foods or the paraplegic confined to a wheelchair, there are two ways to deal with the situation. You can choose to spend the rest of your life growing ever more bitter about the raw deal you have been handed or you can change what you can, accept what you cannot and look for other areas of pleasure. The most dramatic example of this was a lady I knew many years ago. A former professional ballerina, she was so badly injured in an accident that, at the age of twenty-five, she was paralysed from the neck down and compelled to live in an institution where she was lovingly cared for. At first – and it comes as no surprise – she simply wanted to die. Until that moment her life had been governed by movement; she had never wanted to do anything other than dance. By the time I came to know her (which was about four years after the accident), she had taken up painting, holding the brush in her mouth. The pictures she created of scenes from the ballet held a magical quality which reflected the growth and beauty of her spirit. Of course there would always be sadness at the loss of the use of her body – but she had learned that a creative soul can find more than one way of expressing itself.
- You are still you! People are not going to stop wanting to know you because you suffer from a particular medical condition. Initially, unless the condition is immediately obvious, it will be up to you to decide how many people are to be made aware of the situation – and how soon. But, even if you choose to hide it from the world at large, do try and share it with those closest to you. Fears grow more enormous and sadness even deeper when

buried deep within you. Talking about a situation and discussing what practical changes may need to be made in daily life can make things easier to bear – both for you and for anyone who cares for you.

AGEING

Ageing brings its own physical changes and its own fears. The health problems already mentioned seem to become more likely as one grows older. And yet there are many children and young people who suffer from poor health while there are many older ones who enjoy a fit and active 'third age'. A certain amount depends on luck – but a great deal depends on you and your outlook on life.

Physical appearance

Some people (and not only women) do all that they can to fend off the physical signs of ageing. While I think it is important for everyone to try to maintain a state of good health by eating sensibly and exercising regularly, I am not quite so sure about face lifts and other forms of plastic surgery. However it is not my place to judge and if a pinch here and a tuck there makes you feel better in yourself, then by all means go ahead. Stars like Joan Collins and Elizabeth Taylor show that physical beauty does not have to become a thing of the past. Others, like actresses Joan Hickson and Jessica Tandy, who may not have such a glossy glamorous image, prove that a love of the work you do and strength of character bring their own inner beauty.

Mental agility

It used to be thought that old age was accompanied at best by loss of memory and at worst by the onset of senility but, given reasonably good health, this is by no means the case. Einstein didn't do too badly nor did Goethe or George Bernard Shaw. And, although it is true that we do lose a certain number of brain cells every day of our lives, we start off with so many that we have more than enough to keep our mental faculties until the day we die. This does not mean that our mental self does not crave nourishment just as the physical self does. But sensible nutritional care and regular mental exercise will ensure that, failing certain diseases which affect the brain, we will always be mentally agile.

Fear

It is more common, as one grows older, to begin to think about illness or even death. Indeed, no one can guarantee that the former will not come – and the latter certainly will! But, whether you have one year left or fifty, why waste it worrying about what might be going to happen and when it might occur? If you are going to do that, you might just as well give up now. You are not going to be happy and you are certainly not going to bring any joy to those around you. Since that seems a terrible waste of the precious gift of life, surely it is better to do what you can to enjoy its quality. There is also for some the fear of losing their independence. I am not so Pollyanna-like that I can promise this will not happen. But I can promise that it is less likely to occur if you look after yourself in the following ways:

- Ensure you have a sensible diet, adding vitamin and mineral supplements if necessary.
- Take sufficient exercise to maintain or increase your physical strength.
- Use your mind. An unused muscle will lose its strength; an unused brain will do the same.
- Keep contact with other people. If you have the misfortune to be housebound, see if you can find a penfriend to whom you can write. Remember too that, to have friends, you also have to *be* a friend.

- Maintain a positive outlook. Of course there are bad things happening in the world – there always have been. But you have a choice; you can spend your time brooding about these so that you become enveloped in an aura of negativity or you can concentrate on the good – whether that means the caring people who do what they can to help others or the beauty of the sky on a summer's day.

One thing at a time

Whichever aspects of growing older finally come to you, they are not all going to happen at once. You are likely only to have one thing at a time to cope with so that, by the time the next one arrives, you will have become accustomed to the first. How you cope is up to you. You may choose to spend a fortune on 'wrinkle-removing' creams or you may decide that a line or two on the face shows character and life (after all, you've *earned* them, haven't you?) A man may decide to wear a toupée to hide the fact that he is going bald, although it is a very rare (and expensive) one which is going to remain undetected – and baldness didn't seem to detract from the appeal of actor Yul Brynner.

Benefits of growing older

There has never been a better time to be old. At one time sixty or sixty-five was such a great age that there was nothing to look forward to after retirement. Today it is not unusual for men and women to live until well into their eighties or beyond. This means that you may have a further twenty or thirty years to enjoy – no wonder they call it the third age. Are you really going to spend all those years regretting what has gone or worrying about what is to come? There is so much to enjoy and it does not all depend upon your financial resources. You will be able to do as you wish, free of the responsibilities of demanding children. You may choose to take up a new hobby or to devote more time to an old one. You will be able to spend time with friends and family, to travel or simply to walk in the park. You will have control over the way you pass the days – and you are likely to have learned how to experience the greatest pleasure from them.

Whatever the physical changes you may face in your life, be they deliberate, involuntary or progressive, you have it in your power to maximize their positive aspects and to view them as another stage in your own evolvement.

4

Changes in Circumstances

The circumstances which surround us change frequently and how we react to these changes can affect us greatly, both in the immediate and in the long-term. Even those changes which we have made by choice or which bring us pleasure can be unnerving or traumatic – although this can be minimized if we are fortunate enough to be aware of their approach. Those changes which suddenly appear as if from nowhere can (even if they are welcome) cause even more stress to us and to those around us.

Just as they may be involuntary or deliberate, changes of circumstance can, of course, be good or bad. And, as you will have seen from the Holmes and Rahe list in the first chapter, all of them bring a certain amount of tension in their wake. The way in which you handle these changes can greatly affect the amount of stress you suffer and therefore have an effect on your physical and mental well-being.

DELIBERATE CHANGES IN CIRCUMSTANCES

The fact that you have set out to make changes in your life does not necessarily make the situation easier to deal with. Let's have a look at some of the more common deliberate changes in circumstances and see how their negative effects may be minimized.

Move of home

You may have many different reasons for wanting to move home. Perhaps you plan to increase your family or your children are growing up and you need more space. Perhaps, on the other hand, your children have now left home and you no longer need such a large house or want to have so much work to do. Of course, although the move may be deliberate, the reason may be less happy. You could be unfortunate enough to find that you can no longer manage the financial outlay for your present home or you may not feel fit enough to cope with the amount of work entailed in looking after it.

Even if we assume that the reason for the move is a positive one and the decision is one you have made freely rather than one you have felt compelled to make, there may be many anxieties involved.

• There is the sadness of leaving a home in which you may have been very happy and where the memories are good ones. Rooms and houses build up their own vibrations and it can be a real wrench to leave an atmosphere of calm and contentment. It may be helpful to remind yourself that whoever is moving into your house (or bedsitter, flat or bungalow) will have the advantage of entering an already good aura – even if they are not sufficiently aware to be able to recognize it. And, if you have been able to create this atmosphere in one home, there is no reason why you should not be able to do precisely the same thing somewhere else.

    Sometimes it may seem hard to leave when you have done so much work on the house that it almost feels as though you are leaving part of yourself behind. As indeed you are. Once again, look on it as a precious gift to the people who follow on. Perhaps it is part of your role in life to create beautiful settings or delightful gardens wherever you go – and perhaps you are better able to do that than many others would be.

• You may be anxious about the amount of money the move is going to cost. This is where forward thinking can be most helpful. Before you even decide to look for a new home you will probably have worked out what you can afford in the way of a mortgage – but do remember to take the hidden extras into account too. These include such things as surveys – and, if the property you are looking at turns out to be unsatisfactory, you may have to have more than one. In addition there is commission on the home you sell, legal expenses, land registration ... and more. You will also have to pay for the moving job itself and may well find that your new place needs certain basic work (such as plumbing or electricity alterations) to make it habitable. So make sure you have enough money to cover all these items too before you even begin to look for a new home.

- The planning and organization involved in moving home may appear to be a mammoth task. Take things one step at a time. Many of the leading banks and building societies now issue checklists for you to use to ensure that you do not forget any of the essentials – from arranging for meters to be read to insuring your new property. Don't forget to notify everyone – official bodies as well as your friends – of your change of address.

- Are you moving to a new area, perhaps because of a change of job? If so, you will be faced with having to meet new people and make new friends, and some people find this a far more daunting prospect than others. Remember, however, that very few people actually want to be unfriendly or deliberately look for the bad in newcomers. This situation is often made easier for those with young children as parents waiting at the school gate tend to start talking and break the ice. It is also easier for dog owners who often get to know one another as they follow the same route when taking their pet for its daily walk. But suppose your children have all left home and you don't have a dog – what are you to do? Following the same idea – that of being in a regular place at a regular time – you might decide to do any of the following:

– Join a club, society or evening class in your new area;

– Patronize local small shops where your face will soon become known;
– Once you have settled in, offer to help a local voluntary organization;
– If you follow a particular religion, go along as soon as possible to your new place of worship;
– Go for regular walks (even without a dog!) or runs, following the same regular route;
– Invite a group of neighbours to your new home for a drink or a coffee. They will probably already know each other so there will be no long silences while everyone tries to think of something to say.

Making lists

I am a list-maker of long standing, and I realize that this will not appeal to everyone. But I can assure you that lists, particularly if made over a period of days rather than at one sitting, will ensure that you do not forget anything – and it is incredibly satisfying to cross items firmly off your list once they have been attended to! (Mind you, try not to become like a friend of mine who made so many lists that she ended up making a list of her lists!)

In the weeks leading up to the move, make sure that you have paper and pencils all over the place, including beside your bed. There is nothing more frustrating than remembering something just as you are drifting off to sleep or when you have packed all your writing materials ready for the removal men.

Take it easy

I know it would be wonderful if you could unpack all those boxes on the first day – but you probably don't know where you want to put everything anyway. And wouldn't it be marvellous to wave a magic wand and find all the rooms decorated to your taste as soon as you get there – but you know they won't be; anyway, you may be someone who needs to live in a place for a while before deciding what you would like to do to it. Unless you are very rich indeed, you are not likely to move into a home which needs no work done in it at all. So accept the fact that it will take time to get straight and decide on your priorities for the first day. These will probably include: making the beds, having kettle, cups and basic food available and ensuring there is a clean set of clothes for the following day.

Very few people actually enjoy the process of moving and settling into a new home. But if you try and put some of these ideas into action, hopefully some of the stress of the situation will be eliminated.

Getting married (or moving in with your partner)

You would think that the setting up of a joint home with someone you love would be such a joyous occasion that there could be no way for stress to be involved. But any linking of two developed personalities – whether in a business or personal relationship – necessitates a certain amount of compromise. It is also a fact that everything – folklore, television commercials and mothers – seems to lead us to expect that things are bound to go smoothly and happiness is inevitable.

One thing is certain; there will be no shortage of advice for the couple concerned. But, before you act on any of it, stop and ask yourself where the advisor is coming from? In what sort of relationships has he or she been involved? Were they successful and, if so, were they on the sort of terms you would like for yourself? One person may be quite content to play a subordinate role in their own relationship but that does not mean that you would care to do so. Another may prefer an 'open' style of marriage where each partner is free to come and go as they wish – but a commitment of constancy may be important to you. Yet another may have suffered so greatly in their own life that their advice to you is heavily laden with doom and gloom.

So, by all means listen to the words but remember also to look behind the words at the person speaking them.

Even if everything in your emotional garden is lovely, there will still be adjustments to be made to your lifestyle if you are to harmonize it with somebody else's. Here are just a few of the things you might like to consider to help smooth the transition:

- Most problems – and you will encounter problems however much in love you may be – can be sorted out if the people involved will only talk about them. Not only is it essential to discuss things, it is vital that you do so *soon enough*. Once a small cause of dissent or irritation is allowed to take root and fester, it takes no time at all for it to grow to mammoth proportions. Then, instead of being mentioned, dealt with and forgotten, it becomes a source of resentment and is likely to be brought up rather more vehemently during the next argument. So talk, discuss and compromise where necessary.
- However much you love your partner, you are a grown-up individual who presumably has friends and acquaintances of your own. Each of you has the right to maintain regular contact with those friends – and, indeed, will suffer a considerable loss if you allow them to drift away. If you find that one of you resents the time the other spends in other company, or that unreasonable jealousy or possessiveness arises, it would be as well to stop and question the cause of such feelings and what can be done in the way of both reassurance and the prevention of recurrence.
- You are each entitled to your own space – whether you take this phrase literally or as meaning some time on your own. Difficulties may arise when one partner takes the other's need for separateness as a sign that he or she no longer wants to be part of a close and loving relationship. But, particularly in these days when time spent at work may involve considerable pressure and tension, a quiet time is necessary for most of us. It may be necessary (particularly in the early stages of togetherness) to emphasize your need for this space or time of your own

while explaining that it does not mean that you care any less for your partner or the time you spend together. It is important to remember, however, that your partner is equally entitled to such space or time and that you should not allow yourself to resent this.

- It is natural in any relationship, once the commitment has been made, for one or both of you to have moments of self-doubt. 'Have I done the right thing?' 'Should I back out before it is too late?' 'What about those divorce statistics?' Accept these doubts as a natural part of any major change in your life and ask yourself whether yours are based in any way on your parents' relationship.

  If your parents were extremely contented together but were completely different in personality from you and your partner, there may be a subconscious feeling that these differences may make it difficult for you to be happy too.

  If your parents were unhappy or the relationship was acrimonious, you might have fears (subconscious or otherwise) that there is no such thing as a happy relationship and yours is therefore doomed to failure.

  While these doubts and fears are quite understandable – and, of course it is impossible to issue guarantees with any relationship – they should not be allowed to influence your thoughts and emotions too greatly. If you have already thought about yourself and your emotions in the way described in Chapter Two, you will understand why you have become the type of person you are and the subconscious influence your parents and their lives will have had upon you. You will therefore have a greater awareness of yourself and your potential and are more likely to live and develop as a complete individual, comparatively free of external influences.

  Having thought your doubts through in this way, you can then either let them go and lay them to rest or follow the train of thought they arouse and decide what changes may need to be made in your present relationship.

- No relationship, however loving, can survive without mutual honesty. Even when this honesty involves negative comment, this does not mean that either partner needs to be hurtful towards the other. Even if criticism is involved, it is possible to say things in a light enough way for no offence to be taken. But, of course, if you are entitled to be honest when things annoy or upset you, you must also be honest and give your partner praise and reassurance when you feel it. Honesty of emotion is also essential. If you feel particularly loving, say so and show it. So much misunderstanding arises because one person does not actually *tell* the other when they are feeling love. I have heard many people say, during counselling sessions, 'I don't have to say that I love her (or him). She already knows that.' Even if that is true, a little reassurance can do no harm, particularly at moments of vulnerability.

- Never lose sight of yourself. Just because someone else thinks you should change in a certain way, they are not necessarily correct.

When I first saw Andrea she had been living with Martin for two and a half years. Both were in their late thirties and each of them had been married and divorced.

'I have to change; can you help me?' These were Andrea's first words to me. It seemed that Martin considered her 'too soft' and 'not pushy enough'. The situation between them had been growing ever more tense with Andrea trying to become the kind of person Martin wanted while he lost patience with increasing frequency. Finally he had issued an ultimatum – she must do something to become a more forceful personality or their relationship would have to come to an end. So she had come to me to see if I had some sort of magic wand to enable this transformation to take place.

As we talked it emerged that Andrea had always been a gentle, sensitive person. She was not particularly ambitious, preferring her steady secretarial job to thoughts of a high-flying career. She enjoyed the company of friends but would never have been thought of as the 'life and soul of the party'. This had never bothered her and had never caused her any problems in life until Martin made her believe that she was wrong. He thought she should be aiming for a better job with more money and responsibility and that she was too quiet when they socialized with others.

His criticisms of her went on and on. She was too slow at making up her mind; she was too passive, refusing to enter into arguments; too ready to fall in with his (Martin's) plans rather than state her own preferences. And it was all true, Andrea told me. She really ought to be different.

The real problem here was not Andrea's personality or even Martin's opinion of it – although he certainly had a cruel way of expressing that opinion. The question was why Andrea felt that his opinion *must* be right. Why should she change so dramatically if she had always been content with the way she was? And had Martin the right to insist that she did so?

Andrea had never thought of it in those terms. She had been a child who always liked to please others – her parents and her teachers – and, having a gentle and willing nature, had never found it difficult to do so. But the more she tried to please Martin, the more irritated he became with her amenability and the more he tried to change her.

I pointed out to Andrea that it would be possible but difficult to make changes in her basic personality but that it should only be attempted if *she* felt that she ought to be different. You should never try and change completely just because someone else wants you to. She thought about it for a while and then admitted that she did not really want to become more ambitious, argumentative or aggressive. But she was afraid that, if she remained as she was, the relationship with Martin would come to an end. I asked her to think about what there was in that relationship which she found fulfilling or which made her happy – and she was shocked to find that she was unable to come up with a single thing. It had been good enough in the beginning when mutual physical attraction had overridden any underlying problems but she could not say honestly that she had been happy for over a year. She went on from that point to wonder whether she really wanted to change herself in order to bolster up a relationship that did not seem to bring either of them joy. I suggested that, before we went any further, she should go home and work out precisely what she wanted to achieve as I could not make that decision for her – although I promised her that, whatever choice she made, I would do my best to assist her.

Andrea came to see me again about two weeks later. She had done a great deal of thinking and had come to several conclusions:

1. Martin had every right to want to spend his time with a woman who was ambitious and aggressive;
2. Although everyone has to make some adjustments and compromises if a relationship is to work, he had no right to demand such a dramatic change in her personality if it was not something with which she felt comfortable;
3. She did not want to change in the way he wished;
4. The irrationality of his demands had caused her to lose respect for Martin;
5. She did not feel that their relationship was fulfilling enough to be worth fighting for;
6. She would be happier living on her own.

Not only had Andrea come to these conclusions, she had told Martin what she felt and his verbally abusive reaction had only served to reinforce her views. As a result she had found herself a flat, had already moved into it and, with the support of her friends, was beginning to enjoy life as herself once more.

So the important point to bear in mind when it comes to relationships is that, although they naturally involve change on the part of both partners, unless these changes are willingly and happily made, the result can never be mutual happiness and respect.

Change of work

Even if you have worked for it, striven for it, wanted it and succeeded in obtaining it, a deliberate change of work can be quite traumatic.

If you are being promoted or taking another step up the career ladder, there will always be moments of doubt. Have you made the right decision? Will you be able to cope? Is it going to be difficult to settle into a new role?

Your job change may involve re-location to a new area, bringing with it all its own problems of a home move and possibly uprooting a family. Your spouse or partner will have had an opinion about the move and you may well feel guilty if they, too, have been compelled to make work changes because of you.

Deliberate change in work does not necessarily mean promotion. You may have chosen to leave one field and enter a completely different one. Whether you have decided to find work which is more fulfilling or have gone after increased money but a less pleasurable job, adjustments will have to be made. These adjustments too will involve other people – family, friends, new and former work colleagues.

However happy you are with the new work, it is unlikely that it will be perfect in every respect. Perhaps it will be more fulfilling but less well paid; perhaps the hours will be longer or the travelling more difficult. Hopefully you will have spent some time weighing up the probable pluses and minuses before making your decision but there will still be some things you could not have foreseen. Before you decide that you have made a dreadful mistake, sit down and work out the positive and negative results of the changes you have made. Provided the positives outnumber the negatives, you are heading in the right direction and, with a little effort, it may be possible to change some of those negative results into positive ones.

Planning for change

In all the situations described so far in this chapter, the changes of circumstances have been deliberate so you can make plans to a certain extent. There are certain steps you can take in each case:

- Find out as much as possible about the situation surrounding the changes you intend to make. Look at the
benefits but also at the likely difficulties and decide in
advance how you intend to cope with these.
- At each stage ask yourself 'What happens if...?' and
consider several hypothetical answers. For example,
having found a possible new home, 'What happens if I
move into this house?', 'What happens if I stay where I
am?' and 'What happens if I find somewhere different?'
The answers to your self-directed questions will help
you to discover what you really want and to ensure that
those changes you decide to make have been well
thought out and considered from all angles.
- Plan each step of the way as thoroughly as you possibly
can. There are some people who thrive on not knowing
where they will be next week or what they will be doing
tomorrow and, provided this makes them happy, that is
fine. But we are talking here about making deliberate
changes in the practical aspects of your life and deliberate changes often involve a certain amount of planning if
they are to satisfy you. Whether you make lists on paper
or think things through in your mind, you will find it
less stressful to have as many matters as possible under
control.
- Suppose something goes wrong – what is the worst
possible outcome? If you can answer this and realize
that you could cope (however reluctantly) with such an
outcome, it will give you a feeling of great confidence to
realize that any other outcome must be better.
- Be sure that the changes you are about to make are ones
that *you* want and that you are not making them to
please someone else – whether that someone is presently
around or whether you are still trying to please a figure
from your past. We can all put on an act for a short
period of time but it is virtually impossible to live a lie for
ever and, if you are not being true to yourself and your
desires, the changes will not be successful.
- What is likely to be the true outcome of the changes you
are making? What do you hope to achieve – and are your
hopes realistic?

- You have decided you want to change; you have decided what that change should be; you have worked out the various stages involved; now decide what the first step is – and do it.

INVOLUNTARY CHANGES IN CIRCUMSTANCES

Involuntary changes too can, of course, be either pleasant or unpleasant. You may be able to see them coming or they may take you completely by surprise. However they come upon you, the fact that you have not been able to prepare for them or plan them can be extremely stressful – even when those changes are delightful and a cause for happiness.

Pleasant changes

Work

Perhaps you are offered the job of a lifetime; perhaps you are promoted or given a pay rise. Such changes naturally bring joy but they also bring their own responsibilities and these may put pressure upon you.

At first, Ray was thrilled when he was asked to join the Board of Directors. He had worked for the same company for thirty years since leaving school and becoming an apprentice. He had always done his best and had risen to the rank of supervisor of a large proportion of the workforce without losing the respect and liking of the men with whom he worked. The Board of Directors acknowledged this contribution to the company and valued his opinions and, because of this, invited him to join them.

As time went on, Ray became more and more anxious about his new position. All the other members of the Board had been to good schools and to university; they had always been involved in management. It wasn't that he doubted his own ability or knowledge; Ray was terrified of speaking in front of the others because he thought they would look down on his accent and his bluff manner. So, for the first three meetings, he simply took his place and said nothing. It wasn't until one of the senior directors took him on one side to see what was troubling him that Ray admitted his feelings. It was then explained to him that he had been selected *because* he had come up through the ranks and knew the problems facing the workforce and because those with whom he had worked trusted him sufficiently to speak to him and express their point of view. No one cared about his accent or his lack of grammatical knowledge – it was the man himself they wanted.

These comments helped to put Ray at his ease and he was able to be himself and speak his true thoughts at subsequent board meetings. But it is easy to see how, had it not been for that caring and observant colleague, a talented and experienced man might never have been able to fulfil his potential.

Money

We all know that money alone cannot buy happiness but a certain amount is essential if there is to be any quality of life – and a little extra would not come amiss. But, however pleasant it may sound, sudden windfalls can bring their own problems. Whether you have won the pools or Great Uncle Arthur has left you a fortune in his will, there will be decisions to be made and practicalities to be dealt with. What are you to do with this new-found wealth? Should you move, send the children to private school, have the holiday of a lifetime or give most of it away? We could all think sensibly of ways in which to spend a few hundred pounds – even a couple of thousand. But, after the first flush of excitement, really large amounts do not necessarily bring great joy. You have only to think of certain very rich people to look behind the superficial 'fun' of their lives to see that wealth is not the automatic creator of happiness. Not only will there be decisions to be made and lifestyle changes to be contemplated, there are also the feelings of guilt which often accompany a sudden unplanned increase in wealth. Any sensitive person, while being delighted for themselves, will also become all the more aware of the needy of the world. If this awareness makes you want to do something to help some of them, then the involuntary increase in money will enable you to make some deliberate changes of circumstances for others.

Progress

Positive progressive change should always be exciting. It may be steady and gradual or you may suddenly find yourself bounding ahead. But excitement is often tinged with a certain amount of fear – after all, you are heading for lesser-known (or even unknown) territory.

The pupil who is leaving school to become a full-time student may be happy about the forthcoming change and may be looking forward to it greatly; the student who is just about to start that first job; the young person about to leave home and set up on their own for the first time; the former employee who has decided to take the plunge and set up his own business; these are just a few of the people who will understand that the prospect of exciting and challenging changes in their lives is tinged with more than a little anxious anticipation. (The subject of anticipation of change and its effects upon the individual is an important one and will be dealt with in more detail in Chapter 9.)

Unpleasant changes

Until this point we have been dealing with pleasant and positive changes but of course not all alterations in circumstances are joyously received. Those which predominantly concern the emotional self, such as bereavement, divorce and so on will be discussed in a later chapter. What follows concerns the handling of the more practical aspects of change.

Over past years there have been a vast number of people

of all ages who have – often with little or no warning – found themselves made redundant from their place of work. This can never be easy to deal with, whether you are a young person in your first job or a long-serving employee who has been there for twenty years. However much you are told that the redundancies are inevitable and it is not a slur on your character or a comment on your ability – even if the entire firm has closed down so that everyone loses their job – it does not make the situation easier to cope with.

One of the first essentials in such a case is to be honest with yourself about your feelings. Many people try so hard to 'put a brave face on it' that they never even acknowledge their hurt, fear and disillusionment to themselves. But denying your own emotions can be harmful to your mental and physical health. In this regard men seem to experience greater difficulty than women – perhaps because the latter are usually more accustomed to allowing their feelings to surface. The main problem arises when a man with a wife and probably a family is so intent on not worrying *them* that he puts on a cheerful act in front of them. This is quite understandable but, if you are not able to express what you feel to other people, at least be honest with yourself. There is nothing wrong with feeling stunned or saddened by what has happened just as there is nothing wrong with being fearful for what the future might hold. Such emotions are only harmful when you allow yourself to wallow in them. If you are to deal with the situation, initial recognition of how you feel is essential.

We looked earlier at the planning process involved in easing deliberate changes but, of course, this is not possible when those changes are involuntary. In many cases there has been no warning at all; in others, even if the signals were there, we may well have chosen not to see them. This is why, whether involuntary changes are good or bad, it is beneficial to stop and take stock of the new situation.

Whatever the change which has occurred in your life, try making a 'what to do' list. Perhaps you could have a mini-brainstorming session and involve those who are closest to you. In this way you can pay your friends and loved ones the compliment of allowing them to help you. Remember that the idea of brainstorming is to throw in all the ridiculous as well as the sensible ideas. The weeding out comes at a later stage. See how many possible (and implausible) solutions to your problem you can come up with. It is when you reach the point of considering the likely outcome of each step that you will find yourself able to reject the less sensible suggestions. But what is ridiculous to one person may be worth considering by another. 'Emigrate' may not be the most logical answer if you have insufficient funds, you know no one in another country and your family not only live here but all have good jobs. But, if your sister happens to live in Australia, you have a valuable skill, no personal ties and a generous redundancy payment, perhaps emigration is something worth thinking about.

Positive thinking

This is vital if you are going to cope satisfactorily with a difficult situation. It gets you going, enabling you to start doing something about changing the circumstances in which you find yourself and it certainly affects how you act towards others and, therefore, how they act towards you.

Positive thinking is more than abstract hope. It involves playing a positive role in creating your own future. You may choose to use visualization, affirmations, scripting or any combination of the three. You may choose to practise it for yourself or you may feel you need professional help. You may want to do it alone or to involve others. However you set about it, you can be certain that, by changing your mental attitude to the situation which has arisen and your spiritual awareness of the reasons behind it, you can work towards turning any negative change into a positive one.

Michael was forty-three when he was made redundant.

He had been employed by the same electronics company since he was sixteen, working his way up from apprentice to head of a small design department. Then the organization was taken over by a far larger company which already had its own designers – so the entire department which Michael headed was closed down and all sixteen members were made redundant.

Most of the people who lost their jobs had to leave at very short notice but, because of his senior position, Michael continued to be employed in a different department for three months. He had very little work to do but at least he still had his salary and the use of his company car.

One would think, because his temporary job required comparatively little input from him, Michael would have made use of that three-month period to work out what he wanted to do next. But not only did he not seek information or make plans, he didn't even tell his wife what had happened. For three whole months he continued to go to work as if nothing had changed. He was not in the habit of keeping secrets from his family and the strain he placed upon himself by doing so was enormous. He became withdrawn and short-tempered and began to drink far more than usual and his relationship with his wife (who could not understand the reason for her husband's untypical behaviour) became tense and uneasy.

Finally the moment came when he had to admit the truth. One week before the three-month period expired – having had a couple of stiff drinks to give him courage – he told his wife what was happening. Having expected her to be full of anxiety and recriminations, Michael was amazed to find that she was both sympathetic and caring. Indeed she was so relieved to find that her marriage was not collapsing that anything else seemed easily bearable. The only thing she could not understand was why Michael had taken so long to tell her.

The couple discussed the matter at length and decided that Michael should seek redundancy counselling as soon as possible – and that was how I came to meet him.

The first thing we had to do was to help Michael come to terms with his feelings. He had bottled them up for so long that, now the flood gates had opened, he was extremely emotional. He had to learn to accept and acknowledge what he felt and to deal with the stress which had accumulated.

We then decided to make a list of all the plus factors on his side – from the handsome redundancy payment to the various skills he had acquired over the years. Just doing something positive seemed to help Michael think clearly once more. I also arranged for him to take some psychometric tests to see whether he had aptitudes in a direction he had not so far considered.

Next came our mini-brainstorming session when sensible and outrageous ideas were tossed about between us. Michael said, almost jokingly, that he would like to run away from it all and start a small health shop in a country town. The idea was added to the list. When it came to considering everything on the list, I asked him why he had made that particular suggestion. He told me that he had a growing interest in health foods and vitamins and felt that work in that area would be more satisfying than in the cold field of electronics. However, he knew that he would soon feel trapped working in a small shop. But he had begun to think . . . .

The next time I saw him, Michael told me he had applied for a job as a senior sales manager with one of the largest health supplement suppliers in the country. He felt he could happily promote products in which he believed. He had been asked to go for an interview – and this was terrifying him. Having been with the same company since leaving school, he had never had to face an interview before.

Like everything else, interview techniques can be learnt. And, although no one can guarantee that they will get you the job if someone more suitable applies, they *do* guarantee that you will come away from the interview knowing you have acquitted yourself well. So we worked together on perfecting Michael's interview technique, including everything from how to project a positive attitude to ensuring that what he said was backed up by the appropriate body language.

Some days later a jubilant Michael telephoned to tell me that he had got the job! It would mean relocating to another part of the country but this was not a big problem as their daughters were at university and his wife already worked from home. He was to begin next month.

If you can accept that everything happens for a reason – even if we are not able to understand that reason at the time – it makes difficult periods in life far easier to bear. Michael had not chosen to be made redundant and he would probably have gone on relatively contentedly in his job until he retired. But, not only was he now working in an area which appealed to him more, he had realized how much his wife and family loved and supported him and, having experienced the depths of despair during that dreadful three months, he was far more able to appreciate how good life could be. He had also begun to give more thought to his own emotions and those of other people and had become more caring and understanding – another step on the path to spiritual evolvement.

5

Change and Your Emotions

Whatever the changes which may occur in your life, it is impossible to undergo them without your emotions becoming involved – and this is true whether the situation is happy or distressing. How easy it would be to cope with change if all we had to do was work out the appropriate practical responses. Difficulties arise, however, when we realize that our emotions are inextricably interlinked with whatever physical action we may decide to take and it is not unusual for a conflict to be set up within you when your emotional reaction to an event does not match the practical path you believe you should follow.

One very important point to remember, however, is that it is essential to be aware of your emotional responses and to allow them to become involved in each situation. Stifled feelings can cause you a great deal of physical harm as you set up within yourself a battlefield of conflict. Many of those patients who come to consult me about problems ranging from stress to more severe physical symptoms (migraine, asthma, allergies and so on) come to realize during the course of treatment that the basis for these manifestations lies buried deep in some emotional pain from the past. So do permit yourself to feel deeply – both positive and negative emotions – and you may well be saving yourself a great many problems in the future.

71

Deliberate change; involuntary change; progressive change; each of these is going to affect you emotionally, sometimes for a comparatively short time, sometimes for longer periods. The mother-to-be expecting her first child will often feel happy, anxious and frightened all at the same time. The loss of his job may cause the newly redundant worker to feel angry, worried and scared. The student, looking forward to leaving school and starting college, may well be excited, nervous and worried. We do not always have the power to choose what happens to us or what emotional responses those happenings will arouse within us – but we do have the power to choose how much we allow those events and those emotions to affect us in the long- term.

LOVE

There are many types of love; the love between adult and child, between two people involved in a close relationship, between friends who really care for one another, even the love a human feels for a pet. One of the most important forms of love – and the one without which none of the others can be truly fulfilling – is love of oneself. This has nothing to do with vanity or pride; it is the ability to appreciate your own value and to see yourself as a worthwhile and lovable human being. It does not mean that you think you are perfect but, just as we love those closest to us in spite of their faults rather than because they have none, you need to love yourself 'warts and all'.

Perhaps you are one of those people who has never thought about loving yourself – or, if you have done so, you either feel embarrassed at the idea or have decided that you are not really a lovable sort of person. Can I suggest that, before continuing any further, you think about it again. There can be very few people in this world who do not have any good qualities at all – even those generally perceived as villains may be loving and kind towards their own families. Being as honest and objective as you can, decide what are your most lovable qualities.

Write them down so that they are there before you in black and white. (If you cannot find a single worthwhile quality within yourself, you are not really being honest.) Look at what you have written. Whether the list is long or short, can the possessor of those qualities be completely unworthy of love? I think not.

Now make another list. What are the points about you that you do not admire? (And you can be completely honest as no one but you will ever see this list.) If you are particularly self-critical, this list might be a little longer than the other one. But just look down it and decide which of those qualities you would like to change and how you could set about doing so. Make actual plans. What will you do differently in the future to show that you have made those changes? And, once you have made them, will you have an excuse any longer to think of yourself as unlovable? (I am not talking about the odd slip-up to which we can all be prone now and then but about a genuine change in attitude or behaviour.)

Love often involves being vulnerable. If your love is not returned, you may be unhappy or hurt. If the person (or animal) you love dies or goes away, that too can bring pain. But without love (of a person, mankind, yourself or God) you will never be able to experience true joy. Ask yourself which kind of life you would prefer – the one where your feelings allow you to be an active player or the one where you are a passive observer always standing on the sidelines.

Don't, however, confuse love and obsession. Love allows freedom, and love which is not freely given is not love at all. The man or woman who cannot bear spouse or lover to be out of their sight is not giving true love and might do well to think about their attitude to both the relationship and themselves. The person who claims to love God (or Spirit or whatever other word you care to use) but who does so out of fear or as some sort of insurance policy for the future is not being honest – and love has by its very nature to be an honest emotion.

Love of any sort can bring about practical changes in your life. It might cause you to consider marrying or setting up home with a partner or you might decide to devote your life to the care of others. Progressive changes such as ageing may cause you to think differently about love and its value. It is a precious emotion and should be cherished and shared wherever possible.

BEREAVEMENT

The one thing we are all certain to face at some stage in our lives is the loss of someone close to us. And yet it is the one thing we are not taught to deal with – we usually have to struggle through it on our own as best we can.

Death arouses a mixture of emotions and unless each one is experienced during the grieving period, very real problems may be set up for the future. It is only in comparatively recent times that so-called 'civilized' people are allowing themselves to experience grief with all that it entails – the 'stiff upper lip' has a great deal to answer for in the form of stifled emotions and physical ill-health.

The emotions experienced after the death of someone close may vary, depending partly upon whether the death was expected or a sudden shock, but some of the feelings aroused are:

Sorrow

This is perhaps the most expected of the emotions although it may vary according to the circumstances, being intensified if the death was unexpected or the person who has passed away was very young. When we cry – as cry we should – for the one we have lost, we are in reality crying for ourselves. *We* are the ones experiencing the loss – the person who has died is not suffering, whatever your beliefs. If you are someone who thinks that death is the great finality and that there is nothing beyond, there is no reason to be sorrowful for the person who has gone – after all, they cannot be suffering in any way. If you believe that there is a life after this one, whatever you perceive that life to be, then it is presumably better than the one we are experiencing and the person who has died is in a far better place – so we should be happy for them.

This does not mean that we cannot still cry and feel sad at the loss – just that we should understand why we are crying and why we feel as we do.

Anger

Does it seem unreasonable to be angry when someone dies? Nonetheless, it is an essential part of the grieving process and you should not feel foolish for experiencing it. You might feel angry with the person who has died for leaving you behind or for dying without saying something you had hoped to hear. You might feel angry at all those other people of similar age who are still alive. You might even feel angry with the birds for singing or the sun for shining. As long as that anger is given a chance to come out, the reason your mind finds for it is unimportant.

Guilt

Perhaps the commonest and most self-punishing emotion to be experienced after a bereavement. Was there something I should have said? Something more I could have done? Why wasn't I there when the end came? Or (often in the case of the death of an animal – which is still a bereavement) did I do the right thing in having the end induced? If the guilt is not experienced and then let go, the basis may be laid for many emotional problems in the future. So, if you feel you are unable to deal with this emotion on your own and no friend is able to assist you, perhaps you could seek the help of a trained counsellor to take you through it.

Relief

If the death comes after a period of intense suffering, it is quite natural to experience a sense of relief when the end finally arrives. And yet this feeling often brings a feeling of guilt – after all, we are not supposed to feel relief when someone dies, are we? But, if the relief you feel is on behalf of the person who has gone rather than for yourself, then the guilt is unnecessary.

Fear

The death of someone close to you – particularly if that person was the same age as you or even younger – brings thoughts of your own mortality and perhaps fears for your own future. You may begin to be concerned not only about how much longer you are going to live but about the quality of that life. There is nothing unnatural in this but it is important that, rather than attempting to stifle the emotion, you acknowledge it and allow yourself to experience it before finally letting it go.

All the emotions described above are involved in the process of grieving and, for the sake of your own future well-being, it is vital that you allow yourself to experience each of them. Once you have done so, however, put it aside and let your memories of the person who has died involve happier occasions. You have the power to make the choice – once you have been through all the stages, are you going to allow your period of breavement to come to an end or will you carry its burden with you for ever?

LIVING WITH A GUILTY SECRET

When Adam was still quite a young man he was given a position of responsibility by his employers who liked him and valued his work. Finding himself in a situation where it would be possible to embezzle a considerable sum of money from the company, Adam had given in to temptation. His boss had found out but, although he dismissed the young man immediately, he decided (rightly or wrongly) not to involve the police provided all the money was returned.

By the time I saw him, Adam was nearly fifty and had been living with his guilt for all that time. Because he had succumbed to temptation in the past and did not trust his ability to resist in the future, he had never again allowed himself to be put in the position where the possibility could arise. So, for the whole of his working life, he had a series of fairly menial jobs, none of which gave him any responsibility or involved him handling money.

As time went on, Adam's guilt grew within him like a cancer and he became almost a recluse. He seemed to feel that not only was he untrustworthy around goods or money but that he did not deserve the love and friendship of others – he certainly had no love for himself.

It was not part of my job to judge Adam for what he did so long ago – he had done enough of that for himself. My role was to try and help him live a more fulfilling future, free from the stress and nightmares which tormented him. There were several points for Adam to consider:

- He had been trusted and had betrayed that trust so, in that respect, he had failed. There is, however, a great difference between failing and being a failure. If his former employer, a man whom he liked and respected, had felt able to forgive him, should he not – especially after so many years – be able to forgive himself?
- The fact that he had suffered such remorse and so much emotional torment made it unlikely that he would react in the same way again. But avoiding that possibility by evading all responsibility proved nothing. One way in which he could prove to himself that he had really changed and was now someone who could be trusted would be to allow himself to be put in such a position again and to resist temptation. There is nothing clever in saying 'I never steal/cheat/let others down' if the possibility cannot possibly arise.
- If it is true that the spirit progresses by learning a series

of lessons throughout many lifetimes, then he was wasting the rest of this one by not allowing himself to prove that the lesson of overcoming temptation had been truly learnt.

- He was perpetuating the vicious circle of self-dislike by cutting himself off from close personal relationships. As someone who had made a mistake and regretted it, he was probably more compassionate and understanding than many and could well have been helpful and loving to others with whom he came into contact had he only allowed it to happen.

- He was now in a position where he could make choices about his future. He could either continue on this miserable carousel of emotional self-destruction or he could make a deliberate effort to change his life around and do something positive with it.

    I am happy to report that Adam chose the latter path and, although it was not necessarily easy for him, he was able in time to become a more positive and outgoing person.

Guilt is perhaps the most destructive of emotions. Some people inflict it upon themselves ('I wish I hadn't...') while others have it thrust upon them ('If you loved me you would...'). How you react to feelings of guilt can cause you to make changes (whether positive or negative) in your life.

Positive changes grow from looking at the past and seeing the truth of the situation. Acknowledge your mistakes if you made them and determine not to repeat them. Ask yourself whether the guilt that someone else is trying to lay upon you is truly deserved. If not – ignore it; it is their problem and not yours. Once you see situations through clear eyes you can make deliberate efforts to progress in whatever way you choose.

Negative changes arise when you either refuse to look at the past and simply continue to re-experience the morass of emotions it has created or when you allow yourself to be convinced by the words of someone else without taking the time and effort to consider their validity.

FEAR

A certain amount of fear is not only natural – it is healthy. Fear may prevent you walking a tightrope across a deep ravine or dashing into the road right in the path of an oncoming lorry. But when that fear takes such hold of your life that it prevents you making deliberate changes and makes you unable to cope with those which are involuntary or progressive, then it becomes unnatural and stifling.

There are some people who fear all change, however it arises. And what sad lives this fear causes them to lead. Changes are happening to us and around us all the time – whether we instigate them ourselves or whether we are caught up in them. Sometimes it becomes necessary to let go of the past or to take a few chances. If you don't join in the game of life, it is true that you will not lose – but you won't win either!

Many people who are well able to make deliberate changes in their circumstances or even to cope with whatever involuntary changes occur have a real dread of progressive change. 'What will I do when the family grow up and leave home?' 'I dread growing old.' 'I can't face the thought of being alone.' These are the thoughts which arouse terror within them – the seemingly inevitable problems which are going to face them in the future.

Yet the very fact that those thoughts arise should provide them with the tools to do something about it.

- It is no good waiting until you retire to become interested in something other than work. Be sure that you make time for a hobby or an interest well in advance so that you will be delighted when retirement arrives and you have more time to devote to it.
- If you have a family, you know from the very beginning that one day they will grow up and leave home – and, indeed, this is just as it should be. However little time or money you may have and whether or not you work outside the home, it is possible to develop interests and get to know other people while your children are still

young. Not only will this give you a strong foundation on which to build in later years but it will make you a far more interesting person along the way.

- Contact with other people is vital; although it is possible to be quite content with your own company for a percentage of the time, without human contact you will become more introverted and more lonely. Perhaps you could join a group or a club, perhaps you could offer your assistance to a voluntary help organization. Even if you have the misfortune not to be active enough to leave your own home, you can become a penfriend – or, as is becoming quite common now, a 'cassette-friend'.

- You may feel that you are too shy to go alone to a group meeting or an evening class. You might be able to find someone else to team up with but, in truth, you are more likely to get to know the others quickly if you go on your own. Two acquaintances in a group of strangers tend to stick together and talk only to each other and so may never become a part of the general group. And remember that shyness can almost be considered a form of selfishness. The shy person is only concerned with themselves. 'How do I look?' 'Will they like me?' 'I hope I don't blush', and so on. There are three main stages to coping with shyness:

1. Look back to the chapter on Letting Go and ask yourself why you are shy. Babies are not born shy; something has to happen to make them that way. Once you have uncovered the reason, don't let it go on having an effect on you.

2. The next time you go into a room of strangers, look around you for someone else who appears to be shy – there are always others and, because you understand what it is like, you will be able to recognize them. Go up to that person and do what you can to make him or her feel comfortable. If you are able to do this genuinely and wholeheartedly, you will become so engrossed in helping someone else that you will forget yourself and your own fears. You may like to have your opening sentence already in your mind. It can be something very trivial

about the weather or how far they have travelled but, if possible, turn it into a question. That way the other person will have to respond and a conversation will have started.

3. Practise. There is no point in deciding how you will act in a given situation and then deliberately avoiding all opportunity for putting it into practice. Yes, it will take courage – but you can do it. If it helps, do a little visualization (or mental rehearsal) beforehand.

ANGER

We are often told when we are children that anger is a bad thing and should be suppressed whereas, in fact, it is a natural emotion and should be recognized as such and dealt with as soon as possible. Indeed, suppressed anger can cause many physical and emotional problems and the longer this suppression continues the more serious these problems may become.

This does not mean that, the moment you begin to feel angry, you should rush into the street shouting and screaming and hit the next person you see! Although, because physical action which helps you let off steam can often be therapeutic, perhaps you could beat a rug, scrub a floor or dig the garden – thereby helping yourself to feel better and disposing of a boring chore at the same time.

Ask yourself first of all whether the anger is justified or whether you are over-reacting. There is a vast difference, for example, between someone accidentally knocking over and smashing your favourite vase and that same person deliberately picking it up and hurling it to the ground. One merits feelings of anger and the other does not.

If you believe that your anger is justified, you must decide what to do about it.

• You may choose to express it in the form of a complaint. Bear in mind that the way to get results is to *tell* the other person that you feel angry rather than scream it at them. By telling them, you are letting your feelings be known without resorting to aggressive behaviour which is only likely to cause them to be aggressive in return – and you end up with a slanging match.

- You may decide that it is best to walk away from the situation. This is fine provided it is a deliberate and considered choice rather than a means of escaping un-pleasantness. If you are dealing with someone who is never going to understand your point or change their ways, the answer may be to leave them well alone – you don't need such company.

- If the anger has been buried deep within you because of some injustice in the past and it is no longer feasible to express your feelings to the perpetrator of that injustice, then it is even more important that you look at the reality of the situation. Do this through the eyes of the individual you now are rather than the possibly fright-ened or guilty eyes of the earlier you. Allow yourself to feel angry and to admit that feeling to yourself and it will go a long way towards healing past hurts.

JOY

I wonder why so many people find it difficult to express joy or to admit that they feel joyful when they have no problem talking about their negative feelings. Some people even feel guilty at being joyful. Perhaps this is because they are aware that there is so much sadness in the world – and indeed this is true. But, in spite of that, it is not wrong to feel joyful whether that joy takes the form of a brief burst of intense happiness or an ongoing sense of contentment.

When was the last time you not only allowed yourself to feel joyful but took the time to be truly aware of that feeling? And what brought it about? It does not have to be a major world-shaking event; it could be a baby's first smile, a golden daffodil, a beautiful sunset or the release of the Beirut hostages.

Of course you have problems in your life – I am not suggesting that you go around with a silly grin permanently fixed on your face. But there must be something which brings you joy too. In fact, it is often those with the greatest problems who are most able to find joy in the small things. How much we could all learn from them.

Like love and kindness, joy is increased when it is spread around. The more you can pass it on to those around you, the more you will receive. Tell yourself that you have a responsibility to other people to increase the amount of joy in their lives.

REALIZING YOUR EMOTIONS

Every now and then, as part of your own sense of awareness, stop and assess your emotional state. Try asking yourself the following questions:

- How does this fact/event/piece of knowledge make me feel?
- What do I feel about experiencing this emotion (is it a good or bad thing)?
- How can I best express it? You might like to talk about it to someone else, to write it down, to paint a picture – or just to sit quietly and think it through.
- Do I want to keep this feeling or to release it?
- Whatever my decision, what steps will I take to keep or release it?
- What have I learned about the way I really am compared to my self-image?
- How will this knowledge make me different in the future?
- Do I need to take any specific steps to achieve this difference – and, if so, can I do it alone or do I need help?

Your emotions are an essential part of your make-up. Trying to deny them, stifle them or ignore them is rather like leaving one vital ingredient out of a recipe and hoping to produce a delicious cake. All change, whether deliberate, involuntary or progressive, will involve your emotional self so, if you are to live successfully and happily with that change, awareness of your emotions is essential.

6

Personal Evolvement and Development

Every change which occurs during your life is part of your personal spiritual evolvement and therefore has a significant purpose. By being aware of the role such changes play and how they fit in with your own development you can assist the smooth passage of that evolvement.

Because it is a word used in so many different contexts, perhaps we should begin by making sure we all mean the same thing when we talk of something being 'spiritual'. For the purposes of this book, I am not necessarily linking the spirit with the following of any particular form of organized religion. For while some people may have a specific religious belief which has great meaning and importance for them, others have a faith which does not sit comfortably in the pews of one single establishment – be it church, mosque, synagogue or any other.

'Spiritual' in our present context is synonymous with a sense of awareness combined with faith – although it is up to you whether your faith is in something you call God, Spirit, The Higher Consciousness or any other term you care to use. The word itself is unimportant; the belief in something beyond (and greater than) ourselves is what matters. Such belief can help you to be aware of a significance in all that happens – even though you might not be able to understand it at the time.

This is an area where any author can only place his or her own thoughts, feelings and beliefs before the reader for consideration. None of us can offer concrete proof about what happens in this life and whatever may exist beyond it. I can only tell you of the conclusions I have reached after many years of working in this field – although I well accept that in, say, ten years' time those views may have altered slightly as a result of changes not yet experienced.

I cannot believe that this single human life can be all there is. That would seem to me to be an extremely arrogant concept. So, if one accepts that each soul or spirit experiences a series of 'lives', there must be a sense of evolvement and of growth of awareness. Just as the baby becomes a toddler, the child, the adolescent and the adult – learning all the time as a result of what happens to him along the way – so, too, does the spirit grow and learn because of the experiences it has in the different lifetimes.

This does not mean, however, that I believe in absolute predestination; after all, if everything were pre-ordained, what would be the point of living at all? While I find it easy to accept that the spirit may choose the lessons it wishes to learn during a particular lifetime and even that events are so arranged that the appropriate opportunities for the learning of those lessons may occur, it is the individual person – *you* – who either succeeds or fails. This in turn determines whether the spirit can progress to the next lesson or whether the whole thing has to be faced all over again – rather like having to re-sit an exam when you have not gained sufficient marks.

My beliefs are encouraged by those patients who come to consult me for regression therapy. It is possible by means of hypnosis to probe not only earlier stages of this life but to go further back and study some of a patient's former lives. And often the causes of present-day problems are to be discovered in those previous lives when the spirit has perhaps not been able to learn those lessons it had chosen.

I am not trying to convert you to my own beliefs or to insist that I am right. I simply ask you to consider this theory as it seems to give a reason to so much which happens during the course of human life. It helps to answer the 'why me?' we have all asked at some time when tragedy has hit us. Hopefully it will also help us to understand and make good use of those changes which we face, whether they are deliberate or involuntary.

Each change which occurs in life can be looked upon as a learning opportunity and a chance to develop and evolve spiritually. From the great change which happens when you emerge from the warmth, comfort and security of the womb and are forced to face the light, noise and strangeness of the world to the time of the final earthly change when your spirit leaves the body it no longer requires, you are faced with new experiences and new tools for your own evolvement. What you make of them, of course, is up to you.

AWARENESS

Awareness, both within oneself and of the world and all those who inhabit it, is vital if we are to progress. It is the difference between chanting lists of irregular verbs and being able to speak and understand a language. Trying to see the purpose in all that happens develops us as individuals and aids our spiritual evolvement.

Becoming aware that this evolvement exists can colour the way you speak and the way you act. It involves taking responsibility for your own well-being and doing what you can to counteract any imbalance between how you are and how you would like to be so that you can develop your own sense of harmony and inner peace.

Stop now and ask yourself these questions:

- What sort of person do I really want to be? (Don't make the mistake of saying 'would I like to be' as this admits the possibility of failure and, even if there are a couple of hiccups along the way, you are not going to fail.)
- How will I know when I have achieved this aim? What will be different about me? How will I feel?

- What are the steps I need to take in order to become this new me? Dividing a project into stages always makes the end result seem easier to attain.
- What is the first of these steps? (And it doesn't matter how small it may seem – it is still the first step and nothing will be achieved if you never take it.)
- When shall I take that step? If, for some reason, you are unable to answer 'now', then make a commitment for the first feasible moment.

Once you have made your commitment and started on your route, you are bound to fall over every now and then. But that too is an essential part of learning. Failures, great or small, only put an end to progress if you allow them to. There is no shame in slipping backwards or in doing something wrong – only in failing to learn from it. Look at the baby beginning to take a few hesitant steps. When, as happens frequently in the early days, he falls over and sits down with a bump, he doesn't say to himself, 'Oh well, that's it. I'll just have to crawl everywhere from now on.' He may protest or even shed a couple of tears but pretty soon he is up again and having another try. Surely we can be as determined as a baby.

The more you can become aware of yourself and your reactions and the part they play in your spiritual evolvement, the more you will be able to become aware of yourself in relation to other people. Such awareness will enable you to become more compassionate and to understand and empathize with others. Interesting experiments have been done over the last few years when perpetrators of violence have been brought face to face with their victims. Whether the violence was deliberate (as in mugging) or accidental (perhaps caused by reckless driving), true remorse and understanding was rarely present until the victim became to the perpetrator a real person rather than a named statistic. One of my patients who had formerly served a term in prison for a violent attack on a postmistress during a robbery was part of the experiment. He told me that meeting the lady (who fortunately had not been too badly hurt) had shocked him. 'She was about the same age as my mother,' he said. 'It was like having hurt my own mother.'

With the growing concern about world population and the environment, it is impossible to develop self-awareness without at the same time becoming aware of ourselves in relation to the world around us. It is all too easy, however, to think that we should leave it all to *them* – whoever they may be. Of course, governments, industrialists and agriculturalists have responsibilities to which they will hopefully one day face up. But so do we. However small our efforts, their sum total can really make a difference. Whether you collect cans and bottles for recycling, reduce the amount of chemicals you use or refuse to buy products which you know damage the environment, you are playing a vital part in preserving and improving the world in which you live. Anyone who refuses to take responsibility and leaves everything to others surely deserves the world he gets.

Increasing your awareness

The pace of life is so great for many people today that there seems little time to do all we need to do, let alone be *aware* of what we are doing. Everyone is so busy being something that no one has time simply to *be*. And yet, allowing ourselves time to 'stand and stare' can greatly increase our sense of spiritual well-being (not to mention our physical health). So, as you go about your day, try to put some of the following ideas into practice:

- Look around you, whatever you happen to be doing. There is the world of difference between *seeing* your surroundings and really *looking* at them. The sky is blue – or is it? Perhaps today it is a pinkish-grey. Tree trunks are brown – or are they? When was the last time you looked? Most tree trunks are shades of green, brown, silver and grey. The walls of your room may be green – but are they the same shade of green when the sun is shining through the window as they are on a dull day? Have you ever noticed?

- Look at people too. How would you describe those you know best? It is easy to say that Peter is tall, middle-aged, with dark brown hair – but so are thousands of other men. What can you say about Peter which makes him special and different from other people?
- Noise can be pleasant or unpleasant. It is a joy to sit back and listen to a favourite melody and agony when the road outside your home is being drilled. But what about the noises we seldom hear because we are so busy creating noises of our own. Turn everything off and sit still. What do you hear? There is always something – perhaps the ticking of a clock or the rustling of leaves in the breeze. Become aware of those sounds.
- Close your eyes and take a deep breath. What can you smell? We tend to be very conscious of certain smells – the pleasant ones like new-mown grass or the unpleasant ones like stale cigarette smoke – but we probably miss all the more delicate ones. Yet nothing is as evocative as an aroma. Even now the smell of jam-making takes me back to the house where I lived as a child, while a particular brand of suntan oil reminds me of family holidays long ago. As you develop your own awareness of your surroundings, make sure that you include your awareness of the smells around you, whether they are pleasant or not.
- I wonder what your most recent meal consisted of. You could probably list the items for me but did you actually stop to notice just what they tasted like? Did you actually enjoy the food or was it simply fuel to keep you going as you rush about your busy life? Make a promise to yourself that you will savour every part of your next meal, however grand or simple it may be. Sit down, turn the television off and, as you put each morsel into your mouth, be aware of the taste, the texture and of how it makes you feel. I am not suggesting that you will have the time or inclination to do this every time you eat, but doing it every now and then will heighten your sense of awareness.
- Wood can be rough or smooth; grass can be coarse or soft; hair can be wiry or silky; the earth can be dry and crumbly or cold and damp. Allow yourself to become

aware of the textures of the things you touch during the course of your day by thinking consciously about how they feel. Then go one step further and ask yourself what sensations or memories they evoke in you.

Emotional awareness

As well as being aware of tangible things, such as the feel or taste of a particular substance, try and become more aware of your emotions and the fluctuations in them. Try and discover what causes these variations, especially when there is no immediately obvious trigger. Naturally, if someone has just been extremely unpleasant to you, you will understand why you are feeling as you do – whether you are hurt, angry or unhappy. But look for the more subtle nuances in your emotional reactions and try and identify the causes of these too. Ask yourself whether you like the way you react or whether you would like to make some changes. In this way your increased sense of awareness may help you make some deliberate changes in yourself which you might never otherwise have felt necessary. And if you end up liking yourself more, it will have been well worthwhile.

Remember that you have the right and the ability to make choices. You can choose to hold on to an emotion or to let it go. There is nothing wrong with feeling angry if there is justification; but, having experienced the emotion, you must decide whether to do something about the situation and allow the anger to go or to hold on to it for hours, days or even years and permit yourself to feel it gnawing away at you, making you bitter and unhappy, when the reason for it has long since gone.

Suppose, however, the emotion you feel is a positive one – of peace or joy. You will want to be able to hold on to that feeling even when the immediate cause has gone. What is making you happy? Whether it is a specific event (the birth of a child, passing your driving test, falling in love) or something more nebulous in nature (an early spring day or just a feeling that 'all's right with the world'), make a real effort to remember it and the feeling associated with it so that you can recreate the sensation at will. Memories are the most precious things. Whatever happens to you in life – good or bad – and whatever else you may lose, your memories will remain with you.

I'm sure you are perfectly well aware of the wonders of love of every kind – but do remember that it is vital to love yourself too. You are just as important as anyone else in the world. If you do not love yourself and consider yourself a worthwhile individual, how can anyone else? This does not mean that you have to be big-headed or feel that you are perfect but at least by loving yourself you will realize that you are worth working on and so will be able to make deliberate changes in yourself.

If you love yourself, it follows that you must forgive yourself for anything you feel you have done wrong in the past. You cannot change what has gone but you can decide to learn from it and resolve to do things differently in future. Hand in hand with self-forgiveness, of course, goes forgiving others. This can sometimes be extremely difficult but perhaps it can be made a little easier if you try to understand what has happened to make them as they are. I am not advocating here that you should become a 'doormat' and remain in a position where someone else has the ability to go on hurting you in any way and is not prepared to do otherwise. Forgiving and understanding are still necessary if you are not to become bitter and twisted – but self-preservation may still require you to put a distance between you and someone who has not chosen to learn from the past but to continue in the same way.

It is impossible to experience both love and fear at the same time. So, when you choose to feel love (for another person, for yourself or for Life) you also eliminate fear. Which emotion do you prefer?

PEACE OF MIND

Peace of mind is something we all want to work towards. This is not the same as complacency – the 'I'm all right' attitude. It does not mean that we should not do all we can to improve the situation of others who may need our help or that we should not grieve when we are powerless to do so. I am talking about an inner peace which can only be experienced when we have grown to know ourselves and what we want to achieve and are working towards those ends.

Peace of mind is not automatically granted only to the chosen few who have never encountered any major problems in their lives. (In fact, because they may never have had any worries or concerns, and have therefore never taken the time to look within themselves, it may even elude them.) It is often those who have overcome the greatest difficulties – or even those who are still struggling with them – who are able to reach a state of inner peace. None of us would choose to spend our lives in a wheelchair or to know that we are facing imminent death from an as yet incurable disease and yet such people are often more at peace with themselves and the world than the rest of us.

POSITIVE STEPS IN YOUR OWN DEVELOPMENT

You may have heard that aerodynamically it is quite impossible for the bumble bee to fly – its wings are too small and its body too heavy. The only thing is – no one has ever told the bumble bee this and so he flies happily about his business day after sunny day.

Wouldn't it be wonderful if no one had ever told us that we couldn't do something? How many children have heard from unthinking adults such words as: 'You're hopeless', 'You'll never do it', 'You're not as good as so-and-so'. And, because on the whole young children tend to accept what adults tell them, they become the kind of people who *cannot* do something – because they believe they can't.

Think back in your own life. Do you remember such words being spoken to you? Even if you cannot remember them, something must have happened to convince you that 'you can't'. You were not born believing it. And, if something made you believe you could not, you have it in your power to let that something go and allow yourself to believe that you can.

Maureen came to see me because she suffered from anxiety or panic attacks. They seemed to appear from nowhere and at irregular intervals but the results were always the same. First she would freeze and be unable to move; then she would tremble and feel nauseous or as though she was about to faint; finally she would leave wherever she happened to be and rush into the street or into her car and get home as quickly as she possibly could. (She never had a panic attack either in her own car or her own home.) Afterwards, of course, she felt foolish, embarrassed and angry with herself for being so weak. Gradually the fear of having an attack became so great that she went to fewer and fewer places in case the dreaded situation occurred.

In our discussions we were able to establish the fact that Maureen's father (who had loved his only daughter) had been so over-protective of her that he had never allowed her to do anything or go anywhere alone without issuing warnings of the doom and disaster which might befall her if she were not extremely careful. Unwittingly she had convinced her subconscious mind that the only place where she would be safe was within the confines of her own home (and her car was simply an extension of this – an enclosed place which belonged to her and in which she felt comfortable).

Maureen obviously wanted to change and eliminate these panic attacks from her life – and that is why she consulted me. I began by teaching her the breathing and relaxation techniques you will find further on in this chapter and then asked her to practise them regularly at home. She realized that doing this made her feel instantly calmer, although it did not stop the panic being aroused in the first place.

Next we had to decide which situation we were going to work on. The first one should be something relatively small rather than a trip to Australia. Maureen chose a visit to the out-of-town supermarket just two miles from her home as this was something she really needed to do in order to buy food for her family. I asked her to tell me what she was afraid of about making such a trip and she listed the following possibilities:

1. She would find nowhere to park.
2. She would begin to feel anxious while pushing her trolley round the supermarket and everyone would look at her.
3. There would be long queues at all the checkouts and she would be forced to stand there with people behind and in front of her, trapping her.
4. If she had to rush out, leaving her loaded trolley behind, she would never have the courage to go to that particular supermarket again.

We went through the points one at a time and between us came to the following conclusions:

1. The supermarket had a very large car park which only became really full on Saturdays and in the evenings. Maureen would choose a time when she knew there would be plenty of space – say, early on Monday or Tuesday morning.
2. This is a 'what if' situation. I could not promise Maureen that she would not feel anxious while pushing her trolley so we had to decide what she would do if the situation arose.

She would immediately stand still in front of the shelves and practise her breathing exercise until the panic subsided. Although it was unlikely that anyone would actually notice her – they would all be too busy with their own shopping lists – she would pick up a tin and appear to be reading the label so that there would be an obvious reason for her to be standing still.

Once the panic subsided she could do one of two things. If she felt fine again, she could continue on her way up and down the aisles. If she still felt a bit shaky she could push her trolley to the cafeteria which formed part of that particular supermarket, order a pot of tea and sit there until she felt better when she could get on with her shopping.

3. The problem of being trapped in a long queue at a checkout was unlikely to occur if she chose one of the times mentioned.

4. Because she now had a method of dealing with the situation, Maureen would not be forced to rush out of the store and would therefore have no fears about returning.

Once we had discussed all the possibilities, I explained the concept of creative visualization (see later in this chapter) to Maureen and asked her to practise this daily until she was next due to go to the supermarket.

The next time I saw Maureen she told me that she had been to the supermarket twice without experiencing any anxiety at all. And, although I continued to see her for some time so that we could work through her various problems, that was one which never again reared its head.

I was not really surprised that Maureen overcame her anxiety about the supermarket so easily. Panic attacks often arise when the person feels that they have no control over the situation. Once we had discussed every possibility and she *knew* what she would do in each set of circumstances, Maureen *was* in control and there was therefore no need to panic.

My reason for telling you this story is to show that with a combination of logic, understanding and letting go of past influences, and positive self-help techniques, it is possible to overcome quite quickly problems which may have existed for some time.

SELF-HELP TECHNIQUES

We have already looked at the necessity of knowing yourself and letting go of the past. Now let's look at some of the self-help techniques which are available to you.

Breathing

I know you have been breathing all your life – but you would be amazed at the number of people who do not breathe properly. Much of the time we breathe only from the upper chest area instead of deeply from the diaphragm. Since we are talking about awareness, stop and – without changing it – think about you own method of breathing.

You might wonder why, after all these years, you should alter your method of breathing but there are several reasons:

- Inadequate breathing can cause physical pains, particularly in the head or chest. It can also bring about dizziness which would then cause you to breathe even less deeply. From there it is only one step to hyperventilation.
- Shallow breathing means that you only take in about half the optimum amount of oxygen. This has an effect not only on your physical well-being but on your mental agility too.
- If you want to learn to relax or to visualize, correct breathing is an essential first step.

Improving your breathing

1. Stand straight, feet slightly apart. Place your hands over your rib cage with your fingertips just touching. Breathe in slowly, imagining as you do that you have two balloons in place of lungs. As you breathe in, these balloons are inflated as far as possible and, as you breathe out, they go down again. If you do this correctly, you will find that, as you inhale, your fingertips will be forced gently apart. When you exhale they will come together again. Do this for a few minutes until you have established a slow, regular rhythm.

2. As you go about your day, take the time every now and then to think about the way you are breatthing. Feel

those balloons inflating as your ribcage expands and check that the rhythm of your breathing is slow and even (unless, of course, you have just run up the stairs).

Relaxation

If I were able to give one gift to everyone it would be the ability to relax at will. It is well-known that the world is full of stressful situations and that many people live life at such a frantic pace that tension soon accumulates and the nearest they come to relaxing is flopping in front of the television or falling into an exhausted sleep late at night.

Relaxation alone is not the answer to all problems – but it certainly helps many of them. In addition to helping you feel less stressed almost immediately, it is an essential first stage in many therapies. In terms of developing a spiritual awareness of your own it is an invaluable tool. Anyone who wishes to meditate, to visualize, to get in touch with their inner self, to develop their intuitive or healing powers or to be regressed in order to discover past traumas first needs to be able to relax. And the wonderful thing about relaxation is that it is something you can *learn*. And, having once learnt a technique which suits you, you never forget it. If, from time to time, you grow lazy about using it, you only have to start up again for it to be as effective as it ever was.

You can learn relaxation from one of the many cassettes now available; you can join a yoga class; you can learn alone, with a therapist or with a group. Below are two simple exercises you might like to try as a start.

1. Sit in a comfortable chair or lie on a bed (or on the floor if you prefer it). You can have some gentle music in the background if you wish. Close your eyes and spend a few moments breathing slowly and evenly.

Starting with your feet and working upwards, tense and relax each set of muscles. Go slowly, giving yourself time to work on each area of your body in turn. Concentrate particularly on the muscles around your neck, shoulders and jaw as these areas are usually the most tense of all.

Once you have worked all the way up your body, spend

a few moments listening to the rhythm of your own breathing and counting (silently inside your head) 'one' every time you breathe in and 'two' every time you breathe out.

Now picture a beautiful scene – perhaps a hillside, a beach or a mountain slope. It doesn't matter what it is as long as you find it beautiful. The place can be real or a figment of your imagination but be aware of it with all the senses – see the colours, hear the sounds, feel the textures, smell the aromas and taste the air around you.

Remain looking at that inner picture for about five minutes before allowing it to fade and letting yourself become aware of your own body again. Open your eyes and sit quietly for a moment or two.

2. Begin in the same way as in the previous exercise – tensing and relaxing each set of muscles in turn. Now choose a colour which you find peaceful and beautiful – it can be any colour you like and may not always be the same one. Fill your mind and your thoughts with that colour. For some people this is easy to do but, if you find it difficult, imagine a huge paintbrush spreading the colour over a screen in your mind. If you fancy a deeper hue, allow the brush to go over the screen again and again.

Hold on to the impression of the colour for as long as possible and, once it starts to fade, let it do so and then open your eyes. Once again, sit quietly for a moment before getting up.

(You may find this exercise easier if you focus your attention upon something in your chosen colour before you begin.)

Creative visualization

This, of course is a whole topic in itself (see my book *The Elements of Visualisation*) but even a slight knowledge will help you when you want to make changes in yourself.

Visualization entails seeing in your imagination events as you wish them to be – and doing this repeatedly. What you are doing is feeding imagined data into your subconscious until it accepts it as reality. Anyone whose head and mind are filled with negative thoughts is already doing this very successfully – only the wrong way around. The person who wills himself not to fail is far more likely to do so because he is filling his mind with thoughts of failure.

Earlier in this chapter we looked at the problems which beset Maureen and her fears of having panic attacks. Until we worked together on her supermarket trip, she had been successfully visualizing everything going wrong – the panic attack, the people staring, rushing out of the store, and so on. She had used creative visualization so well and so effectively (but so negatively) that she had made the imagined scenario a reality. If it works so well for negative imagery, why should it not work just as well for positive thoughts and pictures?

If you have something which worries you or causes you to feel nervous, practise seeing the situation in your mind with everything going well. Suppose you are someone who hates entering a room full of people you do not know. Practise relaxing and then visualizing regularly, seeing the scene just as you would like it to be. *See* yourself entering the room, pausing to look around and then going up to someone (pick the kindest looking face there), smiling and saying hello. Have your opening sentence in your mind before you start – even if it is something as mundane as a comment about the weather. As the scene unfolds in your imagination, watch the other person smile and include you in the conversation. See yourself looking comfortable and at ease.

Remember you are not *hoping* that this is the way it will turn out. You are watching the way it *is* going to turn out.

Devise a visualization to suit you and your own particular problem and use it daily for at least three weeks for maximum benefit.

Developing your intuition

Here, too, relaxation is an essential first stage. You may be wondering why you should bother about developing your intuition when you have no particular desire to work as a psychic or a clairvoyant. There are several benefits:

- If you are to develop an awareness of yourself as part of your spiritual evolvement, your insight will be greater if you allow your intuition to assist you;
- Whether or not you think of yourself as psychic, a heightened intuitive sense will forewarn you of some of the changes with which you are going to have to deal and will help you to decide upon the direction in which you wish to go;
- When dealing with the past and those things which you have to let go, you are more likely to realize the area of difficulty;
- You will be more aware of those people whom you can trust and those who say one thing but mean another if you listen to the voice of your intuition.

An exercise to aid the development of intuition

Begin with one of the relaxation techniques. Now visualize a door or a gate. It can be any sort of door or gate you like but really *look* at it, noticing the handle, the hinges, what it is made of and everything about it.

Let that door or gate open and pass through. Allow your mind to take you on a walk beyond the door. Don't try and force the images to come; let them take their own time. And don't worry if, in the beginning, you see very little. Just as regular physical exercise makes muscles more supple, so too will regular meditative exercise make your intuitive visualization work more effectively.

Sometimes, when practising this exercise, very clear thoughts and impressions will come to you. At others you might have fleeting impressions which are difficult to analyse. Don't worry about this – but do write down whatever comes to mind as it may make more sense at a later date. Sometimes you will have nothing more than a pleasant ten minutes of relaxation and imagery – but even that will do you good.

There can be no evolvement without change and no change without evolvement. Even those changes which you would prefer not to have experienced and the reason for which you cannot understand at the time may prove to be a vital and worthwhile part of your long-term spiritual development.

7

The Effects of Change

No change, whether deliberate or involuntary, can take place in isolation. Each one brings its own repercussions – and some of these can eventually be far more wide-reaching than anyone might originally expect. It is rather like tossing a stone into a still pool; the expected, immediate and most dramatic effects will be seen and felt nearest the point where the stone landed but the resulting ripples may well be found some distance away.

Any change to you or your life must also affect those around you – just as their changes will have an effect upon you. Of course, sometimes these people provide the reasons for the changes in the first place. In this case there is quite likely to be a knock-on effect; for example, if you decide to change your attitude in order to forgive someone for a past hurt, that difference in you will soon make itself evident and the other person will change in response. And so it goes on – sometimes for the good and sometimes not.

I am not referring only to changes in your appearance, manner or surroundings; the greatest good can often come from changes in your concept of what should or should not be.

It can be difficult or even sad to realize, for example, that you do not love one or both of your parents – or that they either do not really love you or that they prefer one of your brothers or sisters. But coming to that realization can, in the long run, make life much easier for all of you. A parent does not earn the right to be loved simply by being a parent. If he or she has done all that they thought right as you were growing up (even if you now feel that they made mistakes), then they deserve to be given care and respect. Real love, although it goes deeper, does not necessarily make for an easier relationship – whether between parent and child or any other two people. Liking and respect for one another are just as important, if not more so.

If someone around you changes, either through their own effort or simply as part of their own progression, it is easy to misunderstand their motives and what they have become. Because surface changes always reflect deeper inner changes, try and look below the surface and see if you can gain some insight into their reasons. And if you are not sure why things are happening as they are – ask. It sounds so simple yet so many people fail to communicate with each other.

Sandra had at one time been a patient of mine. She suffered from insomnia as a teenager and we dealt with the problem quite quickly and successfully so I had not seen her for several years. Then one day I had a telephone call from her mother, Pam, who asked if she could make an appointment for herself as she now had a problem with which she would like help.

Pam had just discovered that her husband, to whom she had been married for nearly thirty years, was having an affair with a colleague at work. Her husband had promised to end the affair – and had done so – and they were now working to repair their dented marriage. Pam's problem was that she was suffering from various symptoms of anxiety – headaches, bouts of crying, unexplained fears ... and so on – and this was why she was seeking my help.

She told me that Sandra was now married and living about five miles away. Because her route from the office to home took her past her parents' house, she had got into the habit of calling in to see her mother on her way back from work each day. On one of these days she had found

Pam crying and, being naturally distressed, had tried to discover the reason. Pam, not wanting to shatter Sandra's rosy opinion of her father, had told her daughter that 'it was nothing' but that she just needed some time and space on her own. Sandra had accepted this but had left the house almost as upset as her mother.

When Pam told me of this conversation, I asked her to consider what opinion had been formed in Sandra's mind. It was not for me to say whether or not the girl should be told of her father's infidelity – that was up to the parents. But I felt she needed to be told *something* if she was not to create in her imagination all sorts of horrors which might be surrounding her mother. Pam had not, until that moment, thought of the mistaken impression she might have given her daughter and agreed that she would speak to her the following day.

The next time I saw Pam she told me that she had indeed had a talk with Sandra – and was truly relieved that she had done so. She had told her (without going into any details about the affair) that she and her husband had been going through a difficult patch in their marriage – something which the girl, now a married woman herself, could accept and understand. Sandra had then burst into tears and confessed to her mother that she had thought Pam was suffering from cancer or some other life-threatening condition and was trying to keep it from her. Pam was obviously able to convince her that this was not so and Sandra, although sorry about her parents' marital difficulties, was overcome with relief.

That story serves to show how any change in you and your behaviour is bound to affect those who care for you. So, if you know you have changed noticeably, perhaps you should try and give them an explanation – even if you prefer not to tell them the real reason – before their imagination conjures up some terrible tale for itself.

Although, as we have seen, many people are all too aware of variations in attitude and behaviour of those for whom they care, it is amazing how some others fail to see changes – even quite dramatic ones – in those around them. This can lead to situations ranging from the amusing to the serious. A relative of mine, whose hair had been very dark when she was young, decided to lighten it as she grew older. She did not want to go grey and she had no desire to be a blonde; she just changed the shade gradually until she ended up having very light brown (almost sandy) hair. Each time the hairdresser lightened it a little more, she went home to await her husband's comments. Nothing. Not a word. He was so used to knowing her and thinking of her as a brunette that he did not even notice the changes.

Paul's problem, however, was more disturbing. He had never been particularly bright at school and was often way behind the others in his class. By the time he reached nine years of age, the teachers suggested to his parents that he should be tested to see whether he was, in fact, educationally sub-normal. When these tests were done, it was discovered that Paul was totally deaf in one ear and had slightly impaired hearing in the other. This had never shown itself in the home environment as Paul was the only child of older parents and they tended to talk directly to him so that he could hear and understand perfectly. It was only in the class situation that difficulties arose. If Paul sat too far away from the teacher, he heard only part of what was said. And any distracting noises around him would block words out altogether.

It was recommended that Paul be given a hearing aid to help him at school. The results were quite dramatic. He was in fact an intelligent little boy and, once he could hear everything said, his school work quickly improved and he eventually caught up with the others in his class. Then one day he arrived home in tears. One of the other boys in his class had called him 'dummy' and, later in the day, a teacher had said 'Oh, don't bother, Paul. You'll never understand.' Neither of the accusations was true and Paul was distressed by the unfairness of them.

What had happened was that teachers and pupils were so used to thinking of Paul as someone who could not perform well in academic subjects that they had automatically put him into a pigeon-hole and – in spite of the changes brought about by the use of the hearing aid –

there he stayed. Perhaps one can forgive another young child for this failing – but the teacher should certainly have known better.

Pigeon-holing is a very easy trap to fall into and one which we should all make every effort to avoid. If we are to allow ourselves to make mistakes provided we learn from them, then we must accord the same courtesy to other people. If someone makes a deliberate effort to change in a particular respect, then we have to let their past go too and accept them as the person they have striven to become.

CHANGES IN PERSONAL RELATIONSHIPS

All relationships are in a constant state of change; it is unavoidable. Whether it is a parent/child relationship, some other family link, a friendship or a marriage, it cannot remain the same. As we grow and mature and possibly change our circumstances, our way of thinking and our view of the world, we become different individuals. Hopefully the changes in the other person will help us to remain caring and compatible but this is not always so. It is clearly seen in some – though by no means all – marriages which take place when one of the partners is very young. As that person matures it is possible that he or she will want different things from life and may come to realize that, although their partner may be growing and changing too, it is not necessarily in the same direction.

Sometimes, of course, one person in a relationship will try and make changes in themselves in order to fit in more with the other. This is well and fine provided those changes are desired by the one making them. They should never be made just because *someone else* wants it. If, after talking to that person, you really feel that they are right and that you would prefer yourself if you were different in some way – then go ahead. But if you force yourself to be different in a way you do not really want – or, even worse, if you *pretend* to be different just to accommodate someone else – you will eventually come to resent the situation, yourself and them.

Problems also arise if only one person is prepared to try and change while the other is adamant that he or she is fine as they are when this is patently untrue. The answer here is discussion, sharing and honesty right from the start.

Twenty years or so ago I had a neighbour with whom I was good friends. One day she gave me a present – a box of sweets. Now, although this was very kind of her, this was a type of confectionary I did not actually like. But, not wanting to hurt her feelings, I thanked her and assured her that I 'loved' them. For years after that, on every birthday and every anniversary, I received boxes of that same type of sweet because 'I know how much you love them'. What could I say? Because I hadn't been honest in the beginning, I could not suddenly change my story now and so a friend, of whom I was very fond, went on wasting her money on items I used to give away to anyone who would have them. If I had kept quiet in the beginning and simply thanked her for the gift – without the effusive 'loving' it, the problem would never have arisen.

Now I know that a box of sweets does not amount to a major problem in life. But take the same concept and change the situation. Suppose a man or a woman, caught up in the early throes of a relationship, assures their partner when asked that they love sex performed in a particular way when in reality they do not. The partner, anxious to please, will continue in the same way, thinking that he or she is delighting the person about whom they feel so passionately. What is the answer to that one? Does the one who had expressed such delight then turn round and admit to having lied? Or does he or she have to continue to put up for life with something they do not like or may even find distasteful? A little honesty in the early stages, gently expressed, would have prevented either outcome.

If you feel that there is a relationship in your life which is not as good as it used to be – whoever it is with – try asking yourself the following questions. You are not likely to be able to come up with instant answers; they may require quite a bit of thought – but that thinking period could help you gain considerable insight into yourself and the other person.

- What is different about the relationship? Do you just feel different or are there outer manifestations of the changes?
- How long has this difference been noticeable? You may surprise yourself when you think about this one as a change has often been in existence for a considerable time before we actually take notice of it. Ask yourself when was the last time you remember the relationship being as it was when you were happiest with it.
- Can you think of anything which may have triggered off this change? This might take some working out as you have to take into account not only you and the other person but also any external events which may have affected the life of either of you.

At this point, remembering that honesty is the only way to proceed (although honest opinion can always be couched in gentle terms – the idea is not to set out to inflict pain on anyone else) ask the other person the above questions and see how their responses compare with your own.

- What does each of you want from the relationship and what do you feel is missing. Because we are dealing with two separate individuals, this might well be an area where compromise is necessary.
- What does each of you expect of the other? What do you expect to put into the relationship?
- What do you hope to achieve within the relationship and also as separate and complete individuals?
- Having come to a conclusion, what is the first step each of you needs to take to work towards those ends?

A typical example of the type of relationship which could benefit from these questions is that of the parent/child. Let's take a hypothetical case.

Edward is the somewhat authoritarian father of a head-strong daughter, Samantha, who is now fourteen. At that age she naturally wants to go out with her friends, to stay

out late and be treated as an adult. In Edward's eyes, of
course, she is still his 'little girl' and it is hard for him to
come to terms with the fact that she is growing up. In
addition, he is also concerned that she does not neglect
her schoolwork or suffer from too little sleep.

From a very loving relationship, the area between them
seems to have become a permanent battleground. Each is
convinced that they are right – but both are unhappy
because they do not really want to be engaged in constant
conflict with the other. Suppose they were to work
through the list of questions.

- What is different? Instead of talking together as they
  used to, they now argue and shout. Edward tries to lay
  down the law and Samantha often rushes from the
  room, pausing only to tell him that she's not a child any
  more before slamming the door and sulking in her bedroom.
- How long has the difference been noticeable? Edward
  claims it is quite recent while Samantha insists that he
  has never allowed her to grow up. When they really sit
  down and think about it, they agree that it started about
  six months ago but has been growing progressively
  worse.
- What triggered off the change? The main event seems to
  have been when Samantha said she was going to a party
  with some friends on a Saturday night. She did not
  know the girl who was giving the party, who was a
  friend of one of her classmates. Nor did she know the
  address where the party was to be held. Edward refused
  to allow her to go in such circumstances; Samantha
  thought he was being unreasonable and they had a
  terrific row after which neither would bend towards the
  other's point of view.
- What does each want of the other? Edward feels that he
  and his wife should know where Samantha is going,
  with whom and how she is to get home. He also wants
  her to concentrate more on her school work. For her
  part, Samantha wants to be treated less like a child. She
  feels that her father should put his point of view instead
  of simply laying down the law.

- How can they compromise? Edward can treat his daughter in a more adult fashion by explaining the reasons for his demands and listening to her side of the story. Samantha, if she wants to be treated as a more responsible person, should act more responsibly and do what she can to allay a parent's natural fears rather than storming out of the room in a temper.
- What is the first step towards this compromise? Edward and Samantha agree a timetable – perhaps that she will only go out once or twice a week during term time and, even then, will make sure that she does her schoolwork before leaving and is home at a reasonable hour. In return she will be allowed more freedom to go out with friends or to parties at weekends and in the holidays provided her parents always know where she is, with whom and at what time she is likely to come home.

The hypothetical story above is one played out in almost every home where there is a teenager and is perhaps a comparatively trivial example. But the same methods can be used and the same questions asked whatever the relationship and however the problems have arisen to the advantage of both participants.

CHANGES IN WORK RELATIONSHIPS

Whatever your job, if you work with others you will have found that a change in any relationship in the workplace is likely to have an effect on everyone there. If there is an alteration in management policy, all staff are going to be affected. If one individual loses his or her job, the effect will be felt by everyone else; some may find that they have added responsibility (which they might not be able to cope with) while others will perhaps fear for their own jobs and wonder if they will be next on the list. A single disruptive person in any organization can cause arguments and difficulties. People are likely to take sides and ill feeling will prevail, all of which will give everyone a bad name.

Even something as positive as a promotion can cause

problems. The person who is promoted may be delighted or may be fearful that they will not be able to cope or will lose the friendship of their former colleagues. Someone who has been passed over for promotion may feel resentful and jealous or their confidence may take a severe knock from which it has difficulty in recovering.

Alison was delighted when she was promoted to become leader of a research team in the laboratories where she had been employed for some time. A conscientious member of staff, she had always worked hard and tried to do her best. She knew that she was good at her job and was respected by the others in the team (all of whom were men), even if some of them thought her a little aloof.

Once she was involved in the leadership, however, she became progressively unhappy with the situation. There were several reasons for this:

- She believed (rightly or wrongly) that the men who now worked under her resented the fact that she had been promoted over them – particularly as some of them were older than she was.
- She did not enjoy the administrative work which now filled so much of her time. She was quite capable of tackling it but had been far happier when allowed to spend her time working on the actual research itself. This was what she had been trained to do and she felt that her training was to some extent being wasted.
- She felt that she did not belong anywhere. She was not one of the management nor was she one of the team. She became increasingly conscious of the loneliness of her position.
- When the members in the team went out together for a drink, as they sometimes did, it never occurred to them to ask Alison to accompany them. It was not that she was particulary anxious to have a drink or even to go out – it was just that she would have liked to have been asked. On the one occasion she did suggest that she join them, they accepted readily enough – but she never

knew whether that was because they really wanted her to come or because they felt that, as their team leader, they could not really refuse.

Eventually Alison felt that the position was not what she wanted and that even the extra money could not make up for the feelings of discomfort she experienced. She talked to her department manager and was finally given a sideways move which involved her once again in the practical research she really loved.

UNDERSTANDING CHANGE IN OTHER PEOPLE

If you can learn to understand yourself and your reaction to changes in your own life, you will be better equipped to help other people through theirs. This does not mean that you should *tell* them what to do but that you will be more understanding and supportive.

If you have children or are involved with them, you will be surrounded by progressive change as they develop and mature. The more you are able to understand the often traumatic effects of change, particularly when the person undergoing it feels that it is beyond their control, the more helpful you will be to them and the less likely there is to be painful conflict.

If you are married or sharing your life with a partner, then whatever changes happen to either of you must, of necessity, affect the other. Because of this, discussion and mutual decisions are essential.

John and Rachel lived in the south of England and both had good jobs which they thoroughly enjoyed. One day John arrived home and rushed to find his wife. He could not wait to tell her his news. He had been offered a senior position in the company at a much higher salary. It would mean moving to head office some three hundred miles away – but that was not a problem as the company would pay all their moving expenses and help them with the purchase of a new home. He looked into Rachel's face, expecting to see mirrored there the delight and excitement he was feeling.

Rachel was horrified. Naturally she was pleased to hear that the company valued John's work and thought him suitable for a much more senior role. And, although they were not hard up, the extra money would be extremely welcome. What upset her was that it had not even occurred to her husband that she had a job too – and a job she enjoyed and for which she was well paid. If John had told her about the offer and asked her what she felt and whether she would be prepared to change her job, she would have been willing to sit down and discuss the matter. But she could not believe that he had not even thought about it but had simply assumed that she would put her own career to one side and follow his.

The marriage of John and Rachel went through an extremely shaky period after that. Fortunately it was based on such solid ground that they eventually sorted matters out after Rachel was offered an equally good job in the area to which John wanted to move. But had the marriage been less sound in the first place, the lack of understanding John showed about the effect of *his* change on Rachel's life could have caused it to break down completely.

Once you have discovered more about the ways in which changes affect you and are more keenly aware of the feelings of others, you will be able to help and support friends who are undergoing periods of change in their own lives with which they may find it difficult to cope. If you can also help them to understand the concept of letting go, you can ease their path considerably.

Perhaps you know someone who is going through the painful break-up of a relationship. This is never easy and at such times a good friend can make all the difference. Being a good friend does not have to involve taking sides or joining in mass criticism of the former partner. It means being supportive, being understanding, providing an ear to listen and a shoulder to lean on if those are what is needed. The only person who can work the situation out is the one who is experiencing the break-up but, because you understand how traumatic such a change can be in their life, you will be able to empathize and give strength and support.

There is no one who does not experience a bereavement at some time in their life and here, too, you can try to understand a friend's needs – whether it is for silence and solitude or someone to listen to them talking about the person who has died. As we have already seen, a bereaved person will experience a whole range of emotions – rage, guilt, grief, pain – and, because you understand this, you will let them do so and still be there for them. Too many people do not know how to treat someone who has been bereaved. They may say all the right words of commiseration in the beginning but, because they have a lack of understanding of the changing emotions to be experienced, they may soon back away feeling uncomfortable and not knowing what to say or do. A patient whose son had died in a motor accident told me that, after the initial mourning period, people she had thought of as friends avoided her or were embarrassed in her company. One even asked her if she were 'all right now' as though she was getting over 'flu. They did not really mean to be thoughtless or unfeeling but they had no understanding of what it means to lose someone you love and, because of that, did not know how to be a friend at such a time.

While many of us realize and accept that change in ourselves is necessary and often unavoidable, there is sometimes a tendency to want everyone else to remain as we have always known them. Indeed, they do remain the same in our memory and it can be quite a surprise – pleasant or otherwise – to meet someone you have not seen for several years.

Think back now to someone you knew at school – however many years ago that may have been. While you know and accept that you have grown up, developed and changed both outwardly and inwardly, you probably still think of them exactly as they were when you knew them before. Many a forty-year-old has been taken by surprise after a reunion to discover that his or her teenage best friend now has teenage children of their own.

Have you ever met a former sweetheart years after a parting? If so, I am sure that, however pleasant they may be, you will have asked yourself what you ever saw in them and how it was that someone like that could cause you sleepless nights or a broken heart. You have changed and they have too. Perhaps, if you had stayed together, you would have changed together and in the same way, but each of you has had another life, other experiences, other partners and so you will be almost unrecognizable as the people you used to be. So it is no wonder that you can find nothing in common.

Perhaps the greatest gift we can give to those we love and care for is to allow them the freedom to change and develop without reproaching them for doing so. Your children will not necessarily grow up to want the same things from life as you – just as your needs and desires were probably different from those of your parents. Trying to persuade them to fit in with your image of what should or should not be is unfair. Not only will it not work; it may cause them to be rebellious or put on them an unfair burden if they feel that they are disappointing you for letting them down. You may not want to live as they do – perhaps you do not even understand what they want – but they have the right to follow their own path and it is up to each of you to respect the choices of the other.

SELFISH OR UNSELFISH?

Your approach to deliberate change in yourself or other people can be either selfish or unselfish. The selfish person will dig in his heels and insist 'I don't need to change; I'm fine as I am.' If he and everyone else around him are quite happy with things as they are, that may be true. But if anyone is unhappy with the situation, perhaps some discussion and maybe some form of compromise is called for. The unselfish person will realize this automatically.

In the same way, the selfish person will proclaim 'It's all your fault; you ought to change, not me.' *Nothing* is ever completely one person's fault, however much we might like to think so. Once again, if the situation is to be remedied, this should be a time for honesty and meeting halfway. Of course the selfish person, seeing someone else make deliberate changes in themselves or their life-style, might feel threatened and make the accusation 'You've changed. You're different – not the person you used to be' – as though this is necessarily a bad thing.

To outsiders the marriage of Rita and Felix appeared to be a happy one – and indeed it had been for about fifteen years. But then Felix went away on business and, when he returned, confessed to his wife that he had been having an affair with a young woman several years his junior. It was a short-lived affair and one which Felix bitterly regretted. He did not attempt to make excuses but apologized to his wife and begged her to reconsider her instinctive reaction to sue for divorce. Eventually Rita gave in and took her husband back.

How things changed from that day. From being a couple who were able to give and take in everyday life, they assumed quite different roles. Determined to make Felix suffer for his betrayal of her, Rita became dominant and demanding. He, for his part, felt so guilty that he gave in to her over every little thing. So he brought her break-fast in bed every day, took her out for meals, bought her presents and did anything and everything she demanded.

For a while they lived with this change in the relation-ship. But the day came when Felix could stand it no longer. He was truly sorry for his foolish behaviour but could not continue to pay for it for the rest of his life – and he did not like the demanding shrew his wife had become. Rita, while enjoying getting her own way and receiving expensive presents, finally lost all respect for Felix. The marriage ended in a bitter parting and an acrimonious divorce.

I cannot say whether Rita should have taken Felix back after his affair or not. That is a decision which can only be made by each individual couple. But, having agreed to take him back, although their relationship would naturally have changed to some degree, she should have let the matter go. If she felt she was not capable of this, it would have been better to end the marriage as soon as he had confessed his infidelity.

An unselfish approach to personal change comes with the growth of self-confidence and assertiveness – and this important topic will be covered more fully in the following chapter. But, to put it very briefly, the confident person can accept change (his own or others') and will adapt to it in whatever way he chooses – as much or as little as he feels comfortable with.

Of course there is a certain amount of nostalgia in each of us which can almost amount to a resentment of change. Who has not looked at picture books of times past and yearned for the countryside to look as it did? And what about all those tales of how good people were to each other in the old days – 'We never had to lock our doors.' In many cases this may be true – but no one ever looks back with longing at the poverty, the poor health, the death of so many babies or the children forced into labour at an early age. Human memory is selective; it is capable of bringing forth images to delight the senses while covering up less happy occasions. And there is no harm in this. If we gain pleasure from listening to the music of our youth or thinking about times as they were when we were children, then let's indulge in a little sentimental day-dreaming from time to time. It is only dangerous when someone tries to live in the past as if it were still here or when they refuse to see the good things in today's life because they are not the same as the things they loved when children.

Nothing can ever go back to being as it was before – but it can be as good or even better. Fortunately there are many people now who are trying to make sure that it is. After years of neglect, there are efforts to improve the countryside from the point of view of the indigenous wild-life and the environment as a whole. Others are striving to improve the lot of people – whether individuals, groups or mankind in general. Naturally there is still a long way to go but, thanks to the effort of those who are dedicated to making deliberate and positive changes in the world, progress is being made.

Understanding the effect of change on yourself and on other people too helps to create a strong self-awareness and a greater understanding of how you function as an individual. It also leads you to develop a flexible and compassionate attitude to other people – and if we all did that, how much more pleasant the world would be.

8

Improving Your
Self-Image

Your self-image is relevant to the way in which you are able to cope with all kinds of change – deliberate, involuntary and progressive. And, although many people retain the same impression of themselves for years at a time, it is by no means fixed; you can alter it whenever you want. Naturally this takes effort on your part but, if you feel that your self-image is defective, it is something well worth doing. Not only will you deal more effectively with change but you will be able to live a fuller and more satisfying life in many ways.

An improved self-image can help in many ways.

DELIBERATE CHANGE

- If you have a reasonable opinion of yourself and your worth, you will be more likely to make the decision to bring about deliberate changes in your life.
- You will accept that these changes are possible, even if you have to work hard to achieve them. Someone with a poor self-image is more inclined to think that a rosier future cannot be for them as they are 'not good enough'.
- Not only will you believe that the changes you would like to make are possible, you will realize that you

120

deserve their outcome, whatever that may be. If you do not believe in yourself and your own worthiness as an individual, you will subconsciously put obstacles in your own way.

- Once you believe that the changes are possible and that you deserve the benefits they may bring, you are more likely to work wholeheartedly towards achieving your goals and seeing them as a real possibility.

Caroline's early life had involved one tragedy after another. The third of four children brought up in a seaside resort on the English south coast, she had seen her little brother swept out to sea and drowned when she was just seven. The little boy had been her mother's favourite and, after the tragic event, she told Caroline that she wished she had been the one to be lost rather than her brother. From that date onwards her mother had never shown her any sign of affection at all. Longing for love, Caroline had gone out of her way to be 'good', helping in the house, keeping quiet, never causing any trouble.

When the girl was eleven years old her mother, a divorcee, had remarried. Within a year her stepfather had begun to sexually abuse her on a regular basis. When Caroline tried to tell her mother, she was accused of being a liar and a wicked child. The abuse continued, with Caroline saying nothing more about it, until she was fourteen when she ran away from home. Her mother, anxious about what the neighbours would say, found her and brought her home. She then complained to the authorities that her daughter was beyond her control and the girl was taken into care.

At sixteen she was sent out to make her own way in the world. Starved of a loving upbringing and lacking a sound education, the only way Caroline could survive was by washing dishes in cafés and bars and sleeping in a dowdy bed-sitter. When she was eighteen she met Simon, a well-spoken and well-educated young man who was nevertheless extremely insecure, having been continually indulged by his over-protective mother until her sudden death six months earlier. Perhaps the two young people really thought they were in love or perhaps each seemed to supply something the other needed but, whatever the reason, they were married within weeks.

Caroline was soon to find that her married life was little better than her upbringing had been. Simon was a demanding husband in all ways. He expected the house, garden and food to be perfect (although he refused to help in any way at all). He ran his own business as a financial consultant and, having never learned to drive, insisted that his wife acted as his chauffeur, driving him from one appointment to another, sitting in the car and waiting for him while he took clients out for drinks and meals. He was also sexually demanding and, on the occasions when Caroline complained of feeling unwell or exhausted, he had no compunction at all about raping his wife. He was comparatively well off financially and was quite willing to pay all bills – but he would not allow Caroline to work or to have any money at all of her own. She had to ask for every little thing she needed.

Now you may be wondering why on earth she stayed with such a husband. But, as a result of her background, Caroline had developed such a poor self-image that she honestly believed she was getting what she deserved and that she was not good enough to merit better treatment. When Simon told her repeatedly that she was lucky to have found someone to take care of her and give her a good home, she accepted this and did not complain about the life she was leading.

All this went on for some years until Caroline was referred to me by her doctor whom she had consulted for exhaustion and who was concerned about her emotional state. We worked together for some time, laying ghosts of the past and trying to repair her pitiful self-image. Although she had no formal qualifications, Caroline loved cooking and would have liked to learn more about it but, for one thing, Simon did not want her to spend time away from the house and, for another, she did not feel she would be able to cope with a structured course.

Eventually, as she became stronger both physically and emotionally, Caroline began to appreciate that she was a person of worth and value and that she deserved more out of life than she was getting – or had ever had. She applied to a local college for a place on a one-year cookery course for which she found she was able to obtain a grant. She told Simon that she intended to take this course and managed to stand her ground and refuse to give in to his bullying bluster.

The last time I spoke to Caroline, she was about two-thirds of the way through her course – which she was thoroughly enjoying. Simon, like many bullies, had given in when faced with confrontation and had become far less aggressive. Whether Caroline chooses to remain with him in the future is a decision for her alone. But at least now she will make it from a position of strength rather than weakness.

INVOLUNTARY CHANGE

- If you have a strong self-image, you will be better able to cope with whatever involuntary changes life may throw at you – even those which you would have preferred not to encounter.
- You will have sufficient strength and resilience to overcome the problems caused by sudden or unexpected changes whereas someone with a poor self-image will be less likely to bounce back afterwards.
- A positive self-image is often a sign of a reasonably evolved person. You are therefore less likely to waste time blaming other people/the government/fate/God for any misfortune which may have befallen you. You are also less likely to waste precious time and energy in bitterness or despair.
- The negative energy created by bitterness or anger can then be turned into positive energy which you can use to help overcome any situation you do not like and set yourself back on your chosen path again – even if that path is now slightly different from the one you had formerly foreseen.

Take as an example the case of two fictitious men – George and Arthur – both of whom had the misfortune to be made redundant in their early fifties.

Arthur, who has a poor self-image, tends to sit and bemoan his fate. 'It was bound to happen to me' he thinks. 'I'm always the unlucky one.' He looks back on all those occasions in his life when he has not made the grade – from the time when he was not selected for the second football team at school to the day he heard he had been passed over for promotion at work. His future looks bleak as he believes that he has no hope at all of getting another job, he doesn't feel that he has the strength to re-train or to think of setting up some sort of business on his own – he doesn't even have a hobby which interests him. His mind is full of negative thoughts – anger towards his former employers, jealousy of those who were not made redundant and bitterness towards life in general. If he does not re-think his self-image and his attitude, what hope does he have of making a positive future for himself?

George naturally experiences similar negative emotions to begin with. It is only human to think 'why me?' when life deals you a nasty blow. But, once the initial period of despondency has passed, George realizes that, sadly, he is by no means alone and that, although he would have been happier for the situation not to have arisen, it was not a disgrace to be made redundant and did not mean that he was not a good worker with much to offer in the future. He realizes that his age will make it difficult to find another job quickly. He looks for professional advice, discusses matters with his wife and finally decides to take a course at the local college before using some of his redundancy money to set up in business for himself.

The two cases above (unlike the other case histories described in this book) are fictitious. But we all know any number of Arthurs and Georges and it is not difficult to see who it is who gets the most out of life – and I do not mean just financially. Much of it depends upon whether or not you have a positive attitude to yourself and the world – and that positive attitude in turn comes from an appreciation of your own value.

PROGRESSIVE CHANGE

- With a strong self-image you are unlikely to fear those progressive changes which will necessarily occur in all our lives.
- You will be able to look for the good in inevitable and ongoing situations rather than wasting time regretting what has gone. Looking back is fine when it gives you pleasure to relive old memories but harmful when it makes you angry because things are no longer as they were.
- You will have the confidence to do something about a current or approaching situation where this is possible. You will also be more able to re-define your goals when faced with the inevitable.
- It is only the insecure people of this world who really worry about the number of years they have lived or the fact that their looks may not be as good as they once were.

Cosmetic surgery can perform wonders for people who have suffered injury or who have some deformity but, while they have every right to undergo it if they wish, I sometimes wonder *why* some people have the need to remodel faces or bodies for vanity. Do they really think it makes other people like them more? Even in the world of theatre where cosmetic surgery is prevalent among ageing performers, does it really make such a difference? Think of the truly great actors and actresses; they have rarely seen the need to hide their well-earned wrinkles – their self-image has been strong enough to say 'This is me; take me as I am.' And their audiences have done just that.

You are growing older and so am I. There is nothing we can do to change the fact – but there is much we can do to change our attitude towards it. How would you prefer to spend your time: appreciating the freedom you now have to be you – or looking in the mirror to count the wrinkles?

CHANGING YOUR SELF-IMAGE

Before you can do anything about changing your self-image, you need to know what it is now. Refer back to the questionnaire on page 18; what does it tell you about the present state of your self-image? Ask yourself in addition the following questions:

- Do I like myself? If not, what aspects of my personality do I wish to change?
- Am I worthy of the liking, respect and love of other people?
- Do I believe that it is possible for good things to happen to me in the future?
- If so, do I deserve them?

If the answer to any of those questions is 'no', see if you can discover the reason behind it. If you are aware of some aspect of yourself that needs improving, then you are halfway there and can start working on it. If, however, you just have a general sense of not being 'good enough', ask yourself whether this is based on reality or on an image of yourself which has been superimposed by people or events in the past. If it has, and even if it was justified all those years ago, you are no longer the same person. Are you still punishing yourself for mistakes (real or imagined) long since past? If so, perhaps you should work through the chapter on Letting Go again so that you see yourself as you really are and not as someone else once convinced you that you were.

Once you realize where your starting-point is, there are several steps to improving your self-image:

1. Decide what you want. It is important to be specific. It is not enough to know that you want to be 'better' or 'different'. In what way would you like to change?

2. Be sure that you set your goals high enough. If you are someone whose self-image has always been poor, you may well think that being just a little bit better would be wonderful. But you deserve the best – so aim high.

3. Make a positive commitment. Improvements do not

have to begin on January 1st, on a Monday – or even tomorrow morning. Start now! What can you do – even if it is just changing your way of thinking – right now? If there is a real and definite reason why this particular moment is not practicable, make a date for beginning the process – and make it as soon as possible.

ASSERTIVENESS

It is impossible to have a good self-image without becoming a more assertive individual while, to complete the circle, to become more assertive (genuinely rather than by paying lip-service to it) requires a positive self-image. So perhaps we had better look at assertiveness and see what you can do to develop it in yourself.

What is assertiveness?

Assertiveness is the ability to communicate your needs, wants and feelings to someone else without abusing their rights. The assertive person considers himself equal to (but not more or less important than) other people.

The benefits of assertiveness

- If you are assertive you will be better able to manage your time and your stress level effectively by setting realistic goals and limitations.
- You will be able to influence other people (rather than bully them) by stating your feelings and your preferences clearly.
- You will learn more quickly what it is that others are feeling and what they would like.
- The confidence which accompanies assertiveness will enable you to deal more quickly and efficiently with any problems which may arise as you work towards your goals.

- Assertive individuals are more able to work well together and will be more effective as a group.
- Your situation – whether at home or in the workplace – will therefore be far pleasanter and more enjoyable, both for you and for everyone else concerned.

To be assertive you must:
- Decide what it is that you want.
- Ask yourself whether what you want is fair and just.
- Be able to remain calm and in control whatever the attitude of the other person.
- Ask clearly for what you want with no confusion or hinting.
- Be prepared to take chances.
- Be able to give and receive compliments.
- Be able to give and receive fair criticism.
- Say honestly what you are feeling.

To be assertive you must not:
- Waffle or send confusing messages.
- Go behind other people's backs.
- Adopt bullying tactics of any sort.
- Hide your true feelings.

If you feel that you are not assertive, there could be various causes. One is your upbringing. You may have had extremely kind parents but they may have been so anxious to cushion you from problems or difficulties that they made it quite difficult for you to stand on your own feet as you grew up.

Sometimes being the middle child in the family can send conflicting messages. On the one hand, you may receive less privileges than an older brother or sister but, on the other, you are not allowed to be a baby when a new infant arrives on the scene.

Perhaps there were unsettling events in your childhood. Sometimes frequent moves, bringing the necessity of making new friends or starting new schools, can prove disturbing. You may have been sent to boarding school when really you would have preferred to remain at home. Or possibly one parent (or even both) was missing for some time as you were growing up – maybe due to illness, death, army service and so on.

We have already seen how the thoughtlessness of other people – parents, teachers or any other authority figure – can lead to a poor self-image and therefore a lack of assertiveness.

Becoming assertive does not guarantee that you will always win in every situation – this is obviously not always possible. But you will end up knowing that you did everything you could – and did it without trampling on anyone else – so you will therefore still feel good about yourself.

Because assertiveness involves a certain amount of negotiation where necessary, the final outcome may be a compromise but this is not such a bad thing. It does help each participant in the negotiation to feel better about himself.

Learning assertive behaviour is naturally an on-going process but just knowing that you have started will help you to feel happier with yourself and your self-image.

The Personality Types

In this context there are three personality types – aggressive, submissive and assertive.

The aggressive personality

This person can be recognized by the following behaviour traits:
• shouting
• pointing or stabbing with finger
• standing with folded arms
• remaining static

Key words and phrases used include:
• 'You'd better . . .'
• 'If you don't . . .'
• 'Get on with it!'

- 'You must...'
- 'You're stupid!'
- 'Hey, you!'

The submissive personality

This person can be recognized by the following behaviour traits:
- whining
- clenched or wringing hands
- downcast eyes
- stooping

Key words and phrases used include:
- 'I wonder...'
- 'Sorry, sorry.'
- 'Would you mind very much...'
- 'I'm sorry to bother you...'
- 'Oh dear...'
- 'But...'

The assertive personality

This person can be recognized by the following behaviour traits:
- staying calm
- maintaining eye contact
- relaxed pose
- upright posture

Key words and phrases used include:
- 'I think...'
- 'I feel...'
- 'I would like...'
- 'Let's...'
- 'What do you think?'
- 'What shall we do about...?'

Think of the people you know. Some of them will conform to each personality type. Picture an aggressive person;

what can you say about his body language? Now do
the same with a submissive and then an assertive
person.

Becoming more assertive

It is better to start in small ways so forget your major
problems and select a minor one to begin with. It can be a
situation which arises at home or at work. Bearing in mind
the different personality types, how do you react at present? How do you think you should act? What can you do
to make the necessary changes?

If you are not at the moment an assertive person, you
are not going to change overnight. It has taken a long
time for you to become the way you are now so, although
changes will not take as long (because you are making
them deliberately rather than letting them happen), you
cannot hope for an instant metamorphosis. But make
sure that you are sufficiently aware of yourself and what
is happening around you to notice when you improve.
Perhaps you could develop a reward system for yourself so that, when you think you have acted more
assertively, you give yourself a treat – whether that means
a visit to the cinema, a glass of wine or a long, hot bubble
bath.

An assertive person should be able to do the following:

- Express positive feelings:
  e.g. 'I like your hat'
      'I love you'.
- Express negative feelings:
  e.g. 'I didn't like the way you did that'
      'I'm frightened'.
- Say no:
  e.g. 'No, I can't work late tonight'
      'No, I don't really like that sort of food'.
- Express an opinion:
  e.g. 'I disagree'
      'I think this discussion has gone on long enough'.

- Express justified anger:
  e.g. 'You are late again – I feel angry'
       I feel hurt when you . . .'

(You do not have to raise your voice or show other signs of anger to be assertive; it is sufficient to say that is how you feel.)

Remember that, as an assertive person, you have rights. These include:

- To ask for what you want (remembering all the time that the other person has the right to say no).
- To have opinions and feelings and to express them.
- To make your own decisions – but you must be prepared to face the consequences of those decisions whether they are good or bad.
- To choose whether or not to become involved in someone else's problems.
- Not to know something. It doesn't mean that you are ignorant, merely that you have a lack of knowledge in a particular area.
- To make mistakes – but other people have the right to make mistakes too.
- To change your mind.
- To be an achiever.
- To have privacy – remembering to allow other people the same right.
- To make deliberate changes in yourself.

Can you think of a way in which you have abused your own rights in the past? Perhaps you are one of those people who claims 'I never have a moment to myself.' You have the right to some time of your own – whether it is half an hour a day, half a day a week or a week at a time will depend on your lifestyle and commitments.

Being assertive is not just a way of dealing with problems but of making real personal progress. You can decide what you want out of a particular situation or out of life itself and then work towards it. Progress may appear at times to be slow – but as long as there is some progress you can be satisfied.

The non-assertive person plays safe and waits for things to happen while the assertive person looks for what he wants, makes deliberate decisions. He may take chances and he may make mistakes but at least he is doing something. There is an old proverb which says 'He who is afraid to shake the dice will never throw a six.' In other words, if you don't join in the game of life, it is true that you will not lose – but you can never win either.

Giving compliments

Compliments should never be saved for special occasions. Try and get into the habit of giving them frequently. They should, however, be genuine. The desire to compliment someone will make you more alive to their good points.

Because many people are unused to accepting compliments, don't allow yourself to be put off by a negative response. For example, if you say to someone 'I like your outfit; it really suits you', they may reply 'What, this old thing?' but you will have taken the assertive line in paying the compliment in the first place and it may be embarrassment which makes the recipient unable to accept it graciously. At least you can make sure you don't make other people feel uncomfortable when they pay you compliments; you can learn to accept them.

Communication

The ability to communicate well is a vital part of making yourself and other people feel comfortable. The assertive person:

- Is a good listener, realizing the importance of the other person's point of view, whether or not it agrees with his own.
- Speaks calmly.
- Is able to say what he feels.
- Can start and maintain conversations – remembering

that small-talk is important too as it is a way of sharing information and forming a link with another person.
• Recognizes non-verbal communication (body-language).

Negotiation

This is a vital ingredient of assertiveness – and I don't mean negotiation in a business sense (although naturally it is valuable here too).

There are several stages of negotiation. These are:

1. Empathize. Try and understand the other person's feelings and where he is coming from. If he is showing any feeling, make it clear that you are aware of it. For example: 'I can see that this is important to you' or 'I do understand your position.'

2. Ask for clarification so that you both know that you are both aware of each other's feelings.

3. Think of your attitude. Keep calm, breathe steadily and make sure that your jaw is relaxed.

4. Be armed (if appropriate) with facts to support your case.

5. Keep to the point. If the other person strays from it, gently but firmly bring them back to it.

6. Offer a compromise. This does not mean that you are being submissive, simply that there is no sense in stubbornness for its own sake. Two assertive people will soon recognize the quality in each other and will accept that compromise is often the logical outcome of a disagreement.

Dealing with put-downs

Put-downs are remarks made (often by people who feel inwardly insecure) with the intention of making you feel small. An aggressive or a submissive response will do no good as you will feel upset afterwards. However, if you do fall into the trap and respond in a non-assertive way, don't waste time feeling frustrated with yourself. Just decide what you would do on a future occasion.

Here are some examples of put-downs (and what they imply) and some suggested assertive responses:

- 'You're too young to understand.' (You're inferior.)
  – 'Try me and see.'
- 'Haven't you done that yet?' (You're no good.)
  – 'No, when did you want it done?'
- 'It's really none of my business but . . .' (I can make you tell me anything I want.)
  – 'That's all right; I won't tell you anything I don't chose to.'

Coping with criticism

No one really likes criticism even when it is justified. Most of us will respond in one of the following ways:

1. Taking unfair criticism to heart without having stopped to work out whether it was justified or not.

2. Being submissive and making sure that you always agree with everyone else. By not doing anything else you avoid criticism (the no-risks option).

3. Reacting aggressively and snapping back. All this does is start an argument which, if you are not assertive, you will not win. So you will end up feeling disappointed and upset.

Assertive people should not be frightened of criticism as
1. If it is unfair, it is unimportant and irrelevant.
2. If it is fair and constructive, it can be useful to everyone.

There are three main techniques for dealing assertively with criticism:

1. If the criticism is fair and justified, agree and state what you will do about it – but only agree with the criticism itself, not with any judgement which may arise from it.

For example, 'Your bedroom is in a hopeless mess. You're such an untidy person.'

– 'Yes it is, isn't it. I'll tidy it.'

This is not a submissive attitude because such a response depends upon the criticism being fair. Your critic is far less likely to continue as you will have taken the wind out of his sails. Indeed, your ready cooperation is likely to be appreciated and a pointless argument will have been avoided.

2. Suppose the criticism is exaggerated but contains some truth. By staying calm you will remain in control and being assertive means accepting the true part of the criticism. For example, 'You're late. You're always late. Everyone is always having to cover for you. Why don't you pull your weight?' (It is probable that the only true part is 'you're late'.)

– 'Yes, I am late. I'm very sorry. I'll work through my coffee break to make up for it.'

3. Then there is the questioning response which is very useful when dealing with personality criticisms. For example, 'That will be difficult for you because you're so timid.'

– 'In what way do you think I appear timid?'

If the critic is genuinely concerned about you, he will then go on to explain his view. If he is simply being unpleasant, he will probably start to bluster and you will know that his opinions are not worth bothering about.

The assertive way to get something done

If you have ever suffered at the hands or tongue of an aggressive personality type, you will not want to act the same way yourself. But this does not mean that you will never want to get something done so here are some effective guidelines you can follow:

1. Explain what you want. Set out the existing situation as you see it, keeping to the point and being as brief as possible.

2. Acknowledge your own feelings (I feel angry) while empathizing with the other person's (I realize you're in a difficult situation).

3. Let them know what you want, making as few demands as possible and being realistic about whether they are in a position to comply with them. Unless it is totally inappropriate, be prepared to negotiate or compromise.

4. Outline any rewards if the other person complies or punishments if not (I'll take my custom elsewhere in future).

If you can develop a more assertive personality, you will considerably improve your self-image. And, as we have seen, an improved self-image will help you greatly when it comes to coping with changes of every type.

9

The Stress of Anticipation

Anticipation of change can often cause more stress – with all its associated symptoms – than change itself. The nervous driver, fearful of an accident which may never occur; the anxious business executive worried about the possibility of redundancy; the person involved in a new romance wondering whether this relationship is going to work; all these are examples of people whose anticipation of events (which may or may not happen) can cause them to suffer from one or more of the most common stress-related problems.

FEAR OF CHANGE

Perhaps it would be a good idea at this point to look at the sort of symptoms of stress which can arise because of fearful anticipation of change. Those which follow are the most common; if you feel that any of them apply to you – and you know that there is no medical condition which could give rise to them – it may be that you are someone who worries excessively in advance of situations. (You are looking for symptoms which apply over a prolonged period not for isolated instances which can happen to anyone.)

Physical symptoms of stress
Tension in muscles of back and neck
Chest pains

Frequent headaches
Eyes – tired, sore or bloodshot
Constipation
Diarrhoea
Insomnia
Bad dreams
Difficulty in waking up
Excessive desire for food (especially sweet things)
Loss of appetite
Indigestion
Need (as opposed to liking for) alcohol
Increase in smoking
Impotence/frigidity
PMT
Inability to relax
Difficulty in sitting still
Tendency to fidget
Nail biting
Nervous habits
Feelings of nausea
Desire to cry
Heart seeming to race or miss a beat
High blood pressure
Migraine

Mental and emotional symptoms of stress
Feelings of panic or anxiety
Difficulty in concentrating
Sense of apathy
Worsening memory
Feelings of inferiority or inadequacy
Shyness
Illogical fears/phobias
Difficulty in showing emotion
Feelings of being unable to cope
Restlessness
Fear of ill health in yourself or others
Abnormal fear of death
Poor opinion of yourself
Sense of guilt
Inability to make decisions

Feelings of failure
Sense of having been betrayed or let down by others
Belief that others laugh at or make fun of you
Lack of confidence
Agoraphobia or claustrophobia

One of the main problems with stress, of course, is that it is usually self-perpetuating. The more stressed you become, the more symptoms you develop and the less you are able to cope with whatever situation brought about the stress in the first place. It is like a permanent treadwheel and you feel that you are quite unable to jump off. What I hope to show you in this chapter is (1.) how to deal with anticipation of change in your life and (2.) how to break the negative cycle and reduce the stress you are experiencing, whatever its cause. The former is actually easier than you might think because you have already proved to yourself that negative thought works by increasing your stress. So, once you have learned to make it a habit, why should positive thought not work too? And, if it does, you will be able to reduce the amount of stress you experience and, therefore, any symptoms from which you may suffer.

Even the anticipation of happy occasions can induce feelings of stress and inadequacy. There is the worry of entering the unknown and having to cope with things being different in your life. And, of course, the expectation of a bad occurrence increases those feelings many times over. Indeed, it is possible for the person involved to become so negative in thought and outlook that he actually *makes* the dreaded event take place, whereas, had he been a little more laid back about the situation, things might never have taken such a poor turn.

Sheila had never been particularly confident so she was amazed and delighted when Don – a handsome and intelligent man – asked her out. She felt that he could have taken his pick of all the women around and could not understand why he was interested in her. Sensing that she needed a great deal of reassurance, Don did his best to persuade her that he really cared for her, admiring her kindness and sincerity and her gentle nature. When they eventually married, Sheila felt that all her dreams had come true.

Don's work had always involved a certain amount of travelling around the country and staying away overnight. This did not worry Sheila in the beginning but her own lack of confidence soon caused her to wonder whether her husband was always as faithful as he claimed to be. She felt that she could not compare with all those elegant and sophisticated businesswomen with whom he must come into contact. So, every time Don returned from one of his trips, she began to question him about who he had seen, what he had done, whether there were any women involved and, if so, what they were like. Realizing that she was feeling insecure, Don tried to be as understanding as possible. He repeatedly reassured her of his love for her and of the fact that he had no interest, other than a business one, in any of the women he met when he was away.

At first Don always told Sheila the truth about where he had been and the people he had met. But gradually he grew weary of the repeated inquisitions he had to face on his return home and he stopped mentioning the fact that he had come into contact with any women at all, thinking that this would set his wife's mind at rest. Far from it. Realizing that he was hiding something from her, Sheila immediately began to suspect the worst – her husband must be having an affair. She could not let the matter rest but would subject poor Don (who had never been unfaithful to her at all) to constant questioning, even waking him in the middle of the night to try and force the 'truth' out of him.

Not convinced of his honesty, Shelia's doubts grew ever stronger and she became more and more jealous of the unknown 'other woman'. By this time Don was becoming impatient, resenting the fact that he was always being suspected of something he had not done. Instead of coming home, as he had in the early days of their marriage, to a loving and contented wife, he knew that the end of each business trip would bring in its wake another bout of questions and accusations. When he tried to explain to Sheila that she was killing the marriage with her doubts and suspicions, she exclaimed triumphantly that she had been proved right and, for him to talk about the end of the marriage, there must indeed be another woman in the background.

Finally Don could no longer stand the atmosphere in the home and he packed his bags and left – not for another woman but to escape his now bitter and shrewish wife.

Of course, no one can guarantee that any marriage or relationship will last for ever. There may be many reasons for a breakdown or a parting and so it is possible that Sheila and Don would have split up in any case. But it is also possible that, had Sheila's lack of self-esteem not caused her to take the attitude she did, the marriage might have been a sound and long-lasting one. Her anticipation and her anxiety about it caused Sheila to act in such a way that she finally brought about the thing she most feared.

The anticipation of all sorts of changes, good and bad, can bring about anxieties in the mind of the individual. A few common examples follow.

Good changes

Expecting a first baby: You would think that, for most women, this would be a happy and positive time. But because the mother-to-be is entering an unfamiliar situation, all sorts of negative thoughts may come into her mind:
• How will I cope on a practical level?
• Suppose I drop it.
• What if there is something wrong with the baby?
• Will I make a good parent?
• Will I feel hopelessly tied down?
Starting a new job (even when you are delighted to be doing so):
• Suppose I can't do the job properly?
• What if no one there likes me?
• I might be late on the first day.
• Perhaps I'll do something wrong and cause problems.

Moving house:
- Could this be a mistake – perhaps I'd do better to stay where I am?
- The repairs and decorations may cost a fortune.
- I won't know a soul in the neighbourhood.
- Suppose I don't like it there.

Bad changes

If good changes can cause fearful anticipation, the prospect of bad changes can be even worse. The trouble is that the negative person is likely to worry even about things which are unlikely ever to happen.

Losing a job: Because negativity can change your attitude towards your work and your ability to perform well, you are likely to be less efficient if you are constantly worrying about whether or not you will lose your job. And this very inefficiency can put you at the top of the list if the time does come when redundancies may be necessary.

Partner being unfaithful: As we have seen in the example of Sheila and Don, negative anticipation taken to an extreme can bring about the feared situation. After all, a probing and suspicious partner can hardly be a joy to come home to. And some people, when unjustly suspected, could take the attitude that they 'might as well be hung for a sheep as a lamb.'

Growing old: All the negative anticipation in the world cannot prevent this happening to any of us. But the fear of old age can spoil the enjoyment of all the years before it arrives, and that fear itself can cause so many stress-related symptoms that physical and mental health do in fact deteriorate earlier than they might otherwise have done.

HOW TO COMBAT THE NEGATIVE ASPECTS OF ANTICIPATION

There is no point at all in asking you to put the matter out of your mind since this will be impossible. But, if you are going to think about it, make sure you do so in a deliberate and rational way.

First consider the likelihood of the event actually taking place. Naturally, if it is something like growing old, you know it will come. Similarly, if it is a change you are planning – moving house, getting married and so on – then you can make definite plans. But if you find yourself growing ever more anxious about something which *might* occur, stop and weigh up the situation and the possibility of it happening. For example:

Partner being unfaithful:

1. *Why do I think this might happen?*
- He or she has done this before. This is a time to tell your partner of your feelings, without making any accusations or saying that you are suspicious of present behaviour. Being assertive and giving him (or her) an opportunity to reply and explain how they feel, simply say that previous behaviour has made you feel somewhat insecure and that you are in need of increased reassurance until that insecurity has faded.
- You cannot see why anyone should consider you to be special. If your self-esteem is particularly low, perhaps you need to ask yourself why this is so. Look back to earlier times in your life and see if you can find a reason for your lack of confidence. Examine it, understand it and the effect it has had upon you – and let it go.
- It's happening to so many other people. That has never been a satisfactory answer to anything. You and your partner are not 'other people'. You will always find someone to remind you that one in three marriages end in divorce – but that means that two in three *do not*. Why should you assume that you will automatically become one of the negative statistics?
2. *Is this fear changing my behaviour or my attitude?*
- It would be very surprising if it was not! You might react in one of two ways.
   (a) Becoming silent and withdrawn, not daring to speak

about your fears and worries. Perhaps you are frightened to broach the subject in case you are told something you don't really want to hear. But, if you believe that such a change in attitude will go unnoticed, you are wrong. Not only will your partner be only too aware of your withdrawal but he or she might well mistake the reason for it. This in turn could lead to all sorts of new problems – something you could well do without.

(b) Acting as Sheila did in the earlier example and becoming openly suspicious. In your eagerness to discover what you fear to be the truth, you might resort to excessive questioning, bouts of jealousy or even following your partner to make sure all is well.

3. *What is the likely outcome of this change?*

• The probable result of a dramatic change in your attitude or behaviour is that you will drive your partner away – even if he or she originally had no intention of leaving.

4. *What can I do to improve the situation?*

• Think logically about the matter. Do you have any real reason to believe that you are being betrayed? (And the fact that your partner has been late home from work on a couple of occasions does not constitute proof. There can be a sensible and truthful explanation for that.)

• If there is no basis for your fearful anticipation, make a deliberate decision to change your attitude before you drive away the very person you do not want to lose. Even if they do not actually go, a relationship where one person constantly suspects the other is unlikely to be a happy or fulfilling one for either party.

ANTICIPATION OF SOMETHING YOU KNOW WILL HAPPEN

In this case it is often not the event itself which causes fear and stress but how we will cope with it when it arises. Whether it is changing your job or having Auntie Annie to stay for Christmas, it is the ongoing result of the occurrence which will cause you to be anxious. When you know that something is going to happen – whether it is an event you are looking forward to or dreading – start your plans well in advance. Try asking yourself some questions.

1. *What aspect of the event makes me anxious?*
- It is surprising how simply admitting to yourself which are your areas of concern helps to put the whole matter into perspective – particularly if you write them down. Somehow, once you have a list of worries, you feel more able to cope with them.

2. *How would I cope with the worst of those anxieties?*
- Whether it is Auntie Annie's cantankerousness or the fact that you will be a stranger in a new office, there is a solution to every problem. You might decide to look on Auntie Annie's foibles with tolerance and light amusement (or you might consider giving her a large glass of brandy after dinner which will send her to sleep and give you all a rest). If you are to be the newcomer in the office, you can plan to talk to the most approachable-looking colleague and arrange to meet for coffee so that you can get to know each other. This sort of solution will not remove your fears altogether but you will discover that there is a way of lightening the majority of burdens.

3. *Are there any advantages to the dreaded situation?*
- In the case of Auntie Annie, you may have the knowledge that you are providing a lonely old lady with a family Christmas; on the other hand, you may just have to cling on to the thought that she will be going home after a few days! If you are starting a new job, perhaps the money, the responsibilities or the job satisfaction will be an improvement on what you knew before.

4. *What is the very worst that can happen?*
- Auntie Annie's visit may prove to be an absolute disaster and might spoil the family's Christmas. The new job may turn out not to be all that you had hoped or you might not be able to cope with it.

5. *What would I do if the worst happened?*
- You may feel angry or resentful towards Auntie Annie – but there will always be another Christmas and she will not have been able to damage solid family relationships. You might have to re-think the situation with regard to

the job, perhaps putting up with it until you are able to find something else.

- Neither of the above scenarios would be what you would choose but you would survive them. And, if you can survive the worst, anything else must be better. So what are you so worried about?
- And remember, if things turn out to be much better than you originally feared, you will have wasted all that time and energy being anxious and stressed when you could have been looking forward to the impending situation and planning how to make the best of it.

DEALING WITH THE STRESS CAUSED BY ANXIOUS ANTICIPATION

Stress is stress, however caused. It doesn't matter whether the anticipation is of a change you are looking forward to or one you are dreading. It doesn't even matter whether you are right or wrong to be so anxious. The physical and emotional stress which results will be precisely the same, as are the methods for overcoming it.

We have already seen how beneficial relaxation can be in enhancing your general sense of well-being. If you know you are under pressure and suffering from the effects of excess stress, try to practise a relaxation technique regularly until the traumatic time has passed. When things are at their worst, you really need to practise a deliberate form of relaxation on a daily basis. Before you insist that you do not have the time, it need take no more than about ten or fifteen minutes of your day. Surely it is worth spending that amount of time on a relaxation exercise if it can make a great difference to your physical and emotional health. It is even worth getting up fifteen minutes earlier if that is the only time you can find.

Remember that flopping down in an armchair in front of the television – or even dozing on the sofa – is not the same as practising a relaxation technique. It is possible to be slouched (or even asleep) without being truly relaxed. So, for your health's sake, find a time when you can be quiet and alone, unplug the telephone, take off your shoes, make yourself comfortable – and relax. Whatever problems or anxieties you may feel are surrounding you, put them aside for that quarter of an hour. You are not ignoring them or pretending that they do not exist. You are merely setting them to one side and you can return to them once the relaxation session is over.

Sleep

One of the commonest results of excess stress is that sleep – particularly sound sleep – becomes more and more difficult. You may lie there, tossing and turning, with all your problems chasing each other around in your mind. Or you may be so exhausted that you drift into an uneasy sleep, only to wake again an hour or so later and lie there, watching the hands of the clock as they creep towards morning.

Don't worry too much about the number of hours you actually sleep. Some people need seven or eight hours a night while others can manage on far less. The only way of knowing that you need to do something about it is if your normal sleep pattern has dramatically changed or if you find yourself tired and irritable during the day. The occasional bad night will not hurt anyone so try not to let it worry you. If you go to bed thinking 'I *must* get some sleep tonight', you will probably be so tense that you will make things far worse and sleep will evade you altogether.

If you are still finding it difficult to sleep, here are a few ideas which might help you:

- Practise your relaxation technique when you go to bed at night. That way, not only will it not cut into your busy day but it will help you to sleep deeply and soundly.
- There is no point in going to bed if you still feel wide awake so find something pleasurable to do – listen to music or read a magazine. *Don't* use the time to do some

work or to sit and try and resolve your problems or you will never get to sleep at all. Fill the time before going to bed with something you enjoy doing.

- Try and establish a pre-bed routine. You might like to have a long, lazy bath, make a warm drink, or plump up all the cushions; by repeating the same actions each night you will be 'preparing' your mind for the fact that it will soon be time for sleep.

- If you do have that long bath, make sure the water is warm enough to be comfortable but not so hot that it acts as a stimulant.

- Make your warm drink one which is beneficial to you. Tea and coffee contain caffeine and will keep you awake. You could drink decaffeinated coffee but make sure that it is one of those which is 'naturally decaffeinated' as the chemicals in some of the others can be as stimulating as the caffeine itself. You could have a drink of warm milk if you like it or perhaps some herb tea – chamomile is usually recommended for insomnia.

- It is a mistake to use alcohol just before bed to 'knock yourself out'. It may help you to fall asleep initially but you will probably wake several times during the night.

- Have some fresh air in the bedroom. Keep a small window open unless it is *very* cold or it is foggy. Don't smoke (or let anyone else do so) in the bedroom. Whatever your opinion about smoking in general, it creates a stuffy atmosphere in the bedroom which can make it hard to get to sleep and can also cause you to wake up with a headache.

- Hopefully you will have taken some physical exercise during the day – even if it was nothing more than a brisk walk around the block. But try not to leave this exercise until just before bedtime for, although you may then be physically tired, your heart and pulse rate will be increased and this is the last thing you want.

- Because some vitamin or mineral deficiencies can lead to insomnia, it is worth taking supplements if you are finding it difficult to sleep on a regular basis.

Nutrition

We are all becoming more and more aware that the nutritional value of what we eat and drink is of great importance – and this is even more true when you are under stress. So, whether or not you are normally concerned about what you eat, this is a time to take care of your diet. There are many charts available which explain the nutritional values of different foods and the symptoms of deficiencies. In addition to consulting these and making any necessary changes, bear in mind the following minor changes you can make to your diet – ideally on a permanent basis but certainly while the symptoms of excess stress persist.

- Sugar intake should be reduced. Apart from the fact that it contains a great many useless calories, an excess can cause you to become irritable and exhausted.
  - It is now possible to buy low-sugar jams instead of those with a high sugar content.
  - If you use tinned fruit, choose one which is canned in its own juice.
- Too much salt can increase blood pressure to an alarming degree so reduce this as much as possible. A certain amount of salt is beneficial but, even if you were to cut it out completely from your cooking, you would still be absorbing enough from processed foods, such as bread and so on.
  - Use herbs, lemon juice or black pepper to flavour your cooking.
  - Avoid adding salt to the meal on your plate.
  - If you feel you need to use salt, try to keep to natural sea-salt.
- At times of stress try and reduce your fat consumption as much as possible.
  - Forget the frying pan and make more use of the grill.
  - Fresh vegetables shouldn't need butter on them.
  - Whether you use butter or low-fat spread on your bread and toast, try spreading it more thinly.
- Wholemeal products are better for you than white ones.
  - Reduce your intake of white bread, pastry and so on.

- Use brown rice instead of white.
- Choose wholemeal pasta where possible.
- Eat more wholegrain bread.
- Cereals.
  - Make your morning cereal a wholegrain one.
  - Add honey or fruit juice instead of sugar.
- Cakes, biscuits, pastry.
  - Try to avoid these altogether during periods of extreme stress. Keep them for special occasions only.
  - If you feel you must have some, try and choose less sweet types such as scones, fruit bread or tea-cakes.
- Meat and poultry.
  - Avoid red meat as much as possible.
  - Stick to leaner cuts and remove all visible fat before cooking.
  - Remove the skin from poultry before cooking.
  - Try not to have more than 6oz meat each day.
  - Avoid tinned meats or ready-made meat pies.
- Fish.
  - Eat fish rather than meat.
  - Avoid fish in batter.
  - Convenience meals of fish in sauce are not particularly good for you when you are under stress.
- Drinks.
  - Moderate your alcohol consumption.
  - Replace ordinary tea and coffee with decaffeinated and herb or fruit teas.
  - Spring water or filtered water is better than water straight from the tap in most areas.
  - Drink fruit juice rather than squashes which contain chemically formulated colourings and preservatives.

The above suggestions will be good for you at any time but under normal circumstances the occasional lapse will not do you any harm at all. However, if you *know* you are suffering from the symptoms of excess stress, it surely makes sense to try and keep to them as rigidly as possible until the difficult period is over.

You can also aid your digestion and your stress level by eating more slowly, making sure that you actually sit down and take your time to enjoy your food.

Meditation

Meditation is a valuable tool for self-help during a period
of extreme stress, such as is caused by fearful anticipation
of a change or a series of changes in your life. Don't be put
off by the word 'meditation' – it is just taking deep relaxation one stage further. Its value lies in the fact that, as well
as helping to relieve those stress-related symptoms, it can
bring your intuitive side to the fore so that you understand
yourself better and may even be given some insight into
what is really going to happen (rather than what you fear
might happen). If it does nothing else for you, the sense of
inner calm and serenity which meditation can bring about
will certainly help you to feel stronger and to cope better
with any difficulties which may arise.

In order to meditate on the level which will be beneficial
to you in the ways mentioned, you do not have to spend
hours and hours practising, chanting or sitting at the feet
of a master – although there is nothing wrong with any of
those methods for people who want to take meditation a
step further. And, although groups and teachers exist, it is
something you can do quite successfully alone and in your
own home.

The difference between relaxation and meditation is
that, with relaxation, you are concentrating on yourself –
on the release of muscular tension and on your breathing
rhythm. With meditation, however, you learn to focus
your attention on an outside object which may be a word,
an image or a concept. Those who have become masters or
adepts at meditation may be able to clear their minds of all
conscious thought but, unless you have been practising
for a considerable time, you will not be able to achieve
such a state – and it is not necessary for the purpose
described here.)

When observing your outside object, you must learn to
do so dispassionately, without making judgements or
forming opinions. This applies whether you are visualizing something or concentrating on a word or sound.

Meditation will not bring about dramatic changes in you
from one day to the next. It is the constant repetition

which is effective and ideally you should try to set aside a regular daily time (between ten and twenty minutes is all you need) in which you can practise. If that is not possible, try and do it at least three times a week. Some of the recognized benefits of repeated meditation are:

- reduction in physical and emotional symptoms of stress;
- a sense of general well-being;
- improvement in memory and ability to concentrate;
- reduction in blood-pressure;
- slowing of heart and pulse rate;
- improvement in circulation;
- ability to breathe more deeply – therefore improved intake of oxygen;
- better, deeper sleep;
- reduced tendency towards addiction (alcohol, tobacco, drugs, food).

You will also often find that your spiritual awareness is enhanced after periods of meditation, even if this is not what you were originally seeking. You will be able to put episodes of your present life into perspective, seeing the reasons for the changes which have occurred. You may also find it easier to see this life as part of the progress of your spirit on its journey towards perfection.

How to meditate

When you begin, it is a good idea to practise at the same time and in the same place on each occasion. After you have been meditating for some time, you will find this less important. It is best to refrain from eating or drinking anything for about twenty minutes prior to meditating – and you should certainly avoid alcohol for at least an hour before.

There are many ways of meditation – probably as many as there are teachers of the technique. As time goes by you will begin to evolve your own method but here are two which work and so will make a good starting point:

1. Sit in a comfortable chair, making sure that your back and your neck are supported. Close your eyes and begin by practising the relaxation method to which you have become accustomed.

Now, as you sit there quietly, imagine an object of your choice. Keep it quite simple – a single flower, a tree, a burning candle. Try and concentrate on that object to the exclusion of everything else. You are bound to find this difficult in the beginning but don't worry if your thoughts begin to stray – and don't spoil the moment by allowing yourself to become impatient or irritated. Simply put the intrusive thought from your mind and return again to your chosen object.

See the object in your mind's eye in as much detail as possible. If it is a flower, what colour is it? What shape are the petals? Are there any leaves on the stem? Is the flower a bud or fully open? Stay with the image for as long as possible – which may not be very long in the beginning but you will improve with practice. When you have finished, say a silent 'thank you' for the peace you have been shown and open your eyes. Wait a few moments before resuming your normal routine.

2. Before you begin, choose for yourself a mantra. A mantra is simply a word or sound on which to focus while meditating. You may prefer to use a word you like (such as 'peace') or you might like to use one which includes a humming sound (like 'sun' or 'moon'). Some people use a humming sound which has no particular meaning ('omm', 'umm', and so on).

Once again, sit comfortably, close your eyes and practise your chosen relaxation technique.

Now repeat the word to yourself over and over again. You can actually say it aloud or you can just think it to yourself and repeat it inside your head. Eventually you will become aware of how the word sounds and feels and its meaning will be quite unimportant.

Meditation is a valuable technique which, once you have become used to it, can be practised anywhere at any time – travelling in a train or relaxing on the beach. It will not of itself bring about dramatic changes in your life but it will certainly help you to deal with those which arise spontaneously and perhaps to be more in control of those changes you wish to make deliberately.

Visualization

We have mentioned visualization before but, when dealing with the anticipation of change, the ability to rehearse in your mind what is going to occur can be of inestimable help. Whether those changes are to be deliberate, involuntary or progressive, the ability to 'see' the resulting situations in advance can forearm you so that you are able to deal with the difficulties. It can also reduce the fear of what may be approaching because you will already have faced it in your imagination.

If you are someone who worries a great deal, then you are already visualizing beautifully. The problem is that you are visualizing in a negative way, preparing yourself for the worst and imagining it actually happening. If you can turn that same talent around so that you develop the ability to visualize positively and creatively, you will give yourself present equanimity and ability in the future to deal with whatever may arise. This will greatly reduce any stress you may be suffering because of the anxiety caused by anticipation.

Deliberate change

If the change ahead is one you intend to make for yourself, you can use visualization in several ways.

If you know that a change is necessary but you are unsure about the direction you should take, list the possibilities and spend some time visualizing each, together with the likely results, and see where each one would lead you. Because visualization incorporates a relaxation technique and allows your subconscious to play its part too, you will be more likely to be able to use your intuition when deciding which route to follow.

If there is no choice and there is only one direction in which you can go, use visualization to give you the chance to 'practise' following the inevitable path and reacting positively to each step of the way.

For example, suppose you are due to go for an interview for a new job. Many people do badly at interviews because they are so nervous that they do not come across at their best. Perhaps they have not been able to sleep for a couple of nights beforehand or maybe their personal self-esteem is so low that they assume all the other candidates must be better than they are and therefore more suited to the job. What can you do to counteract this? (I am assuming that you will already have done the practical things like finding out about the company, ensuring that you have a satisfactory CV and so on.)

- If possible, start about three weeks before the interview is to take place – or, if you do not know about it three weeks in advance, give yourself as much time as possible.
- Every night in bed, immediately prior to going to sleep, practise your relaxation technique and then 'see' the interview in your imagination, making sure that everything goes as you would wish. You look right; your attitude is perfect; the interviewer asks you questions which you are well able to answer; you are confident and in control with no sign of nerves at all.
- Remember that, because you are doing this in your imagination, you are in complete control and so you can *make* it all happen perfectly. If you find that any negative thoughts creep in, stop and put them to one side and then return to your visualization.
- What you are doing is creating a new programme in your subconscious mind. In the past it has been your subconscious which has convinced you that you are not good enough or that you are bound to fail. But, just as you can record over an audio or video cassette or a computer disk, you can also 'record over' the message

imprinted on your subconscious so that it grows to accept that you are the positive, successful person you would like to be.

- Continue in the same way every night until the day of the interview itself. By then, your subconscious mind will believe in your ability and you will act in the way you have been imagining. Naturally this cannot guarantee that you will get the job for which you have applied – there may be someone else with far more experience – but it does ensure that you will not fail because you let yourself down at the interview and that you will not come away feeling that you have done badly or that it was your fault that you did not succeed.

- Once you know that you can handle interviews successfully, use the same technique for any one which may be arranged and, as soon as you find the position for which you are the most suitable candidate, you are bound to be offered it.

Involuntary change

The way to use visualization when dealing with involuntary change depends on whether or not you have advance warning of the change itself. If you are to have an operation or be made redundant, you will know that the situation is approaching and can start to deal with it in advance. If you have the misfortune to have an accident, then, of course, you do not have the advance notice and may not even be in a fit state to use visualization immediately.

1. If you know about the approaching change, even if it is not one you would have chosen, you have time to use visualization methods to work out the results and thus reduce the fear and stress caused by being thrown into the unknown. Whatever the circumstance, try to visualize all the different possible outcomes from the best to the worst – only make sure that you are logical when it comes to imagining the worst scenario; I can think of very few

situations where you would actually find yourself sitting in the street with nowhere to go unless you had contributed to that state. Even those who have the misfortune to lose their homes are given some sort of roof over their heads – although I realize it might not be the roof they would have chosen. But, if that is the very worst and you could survive it, anything else you face must be better.

This is the reason for imagining every possible outcome of an involuntary change. Once you have faced up to the worst one and realize that you would survive, the greatest fears are often removed. Having done that, concentrate on visualizing a more successful result of the change and it is far more likely to occur for the following reasons:

- The power of thought is very real and you may be able to influence future events more than you think;
- Concentrating on something good is likely to make you more positive as an individual and therefore more able to take advantage of any possibilities which come your way;
- Repeated relaxation and positive visualization will reduce the stress of the situation so that you feel better in yourself and are less likely to suffer a stress-related illness which would render you less able to cope.

2. If the change takes you by surprise, as in the case of an accident, there may be very little you can do as it occurs. But, as soon as you are in a fit state to do so, practise visualizing a return to normal as soon as possible. Not only will this actually improve your physical condition by regulating pulse, blood pressure, flow of adrenaline and so on, but there is a great deal of evidence to support the fact that those who believe they are going to make a full and speedy recovery are far more likely to do so.

Progressive change

Because, much as you may like to push the thoughts to the back of your mind, you know in advance that progressive changes are going to take place, you can prepare for them and for a positive outcome in advance by working on them just as you would when visualizing the result of any involuntary change of which you have prior knowledge. Once again, visualization can help to throw off fears and increase the possibility of all going well.

Seeking help

It is only in the last few years that people have been able to seek help for stress and its related symptoms without feeling that they are being foolish or might appear inadequate. And yet stress is a condition just as much as earache; you would have no hesitation in asking for help from a professional for the latter – why worry about the former?

There are various therapists you can consult about stress, both physical and emotional. Or you can join a self-help group or work on yourself using one of the many books or cassettes available.

Massage

Massage can be most helpful in counteracting the build-up of stress. Obviously the masseur will work on the muscles of your body but the emotional results can be just as positive. By reducing physical tension, massage can reduce the excessive activity of the central nervous system and can, therefore, release you from the vicious circle of stress-tension-anxiety-stress. In addition, the warmth of human contact and touch reawakens those feelings of peace and security we may not have experienced since babyhood. It has been found that adults who can give and receive touch freely have greater confidence and a higher self-esteem than those who are unable to do so.

Aromatherapy is a form of massage using essential oils made from natural sources. It is relaxing and therapeutic and a qualified aromatherapist will be willing to create a special blend of those oils most appropriate to your needs.

Shiatsu is a healing method which originated in Japan. It requires pressure on acupuncture points using fingers, thumbs and palms as well as elbows and knees – although it is not as violent as it sounds. It releases tension as well as working on specific conditions and should always be practised by a skilled and qualified practitioner.

Hypnotherapy

Since the first stage of hypnosis is deep relaxation, hypnotherapy is very effective in counteracting stress. A trained therapist can then go on to help you overcome such resulting problems as migraine, insomnia, high blood pressure, lack of confidence, anxiety – and many others. In the distant past, hypnotherapy was associated in the minds of many people with such characters as Svengali – someone who was able completely to control the subjects. Fortunately it is now widely recognized, both by the general public and many members of the medical profession, that this is not the only side to it and that hypnotherapy can be both effective and beneficial.

Yoga

Regular practice of yoga can bring about a feeling of serenity and a freedom from stress – and you do not have to be able to stand on your head or tie yourself in knots to achieve this. Yoga strives to restore the natural balance of mind, body and spirit. It can be taught individually or within groups and there are also a number of yoga cassettes generally available for personal use.

Whatever form of therapeutic help you might seek, it is essential to consult a qualified practitioner who will be bound by a recognized code of ethics. Should you have difficulty in finding one, you will find in the Appendix addresses of some of the governing bodies or training establishments of the various therapies, any of whom would be able to send you details of practitioners in your own area.

Appendix

Books

Kenton, L. Stress and Relaxation, Century Hutchinson, 1986.

Markham, U. The Elements of Visualisation, Element Books, 1989.

Markham, U. Hypnosis, Optima, 1987.

Norfolk, D. Fit For Life, Hamlyn, 1980.

Pietroni, P. Holistic Living, Dent, 1986.

Cassettes for relaxation and hypnotherapy from
The Hypnothink Foundation
PO Box 154
Cheltenham, Glos.
GL53 9EG

Thorsons Publishing Group
78–85 Fulham Palace Road
London W6 8 JB

Organizations
(please include a stamped addressed envelope with any enquiry)

British School of Yoga
24 Osney Crescent
Paignton, Devon
TQ4 5EY

Hypnotherapy Register
The Hypnothink Foundation
PO Box 154
Cheltenham, Glos.
GL53 9EG

London College of Massage & Shiatsu
6 Claribel Road
London SW9 6TH

Tisserand Aromatherapy Institute
Linkline House
65 Church Road
Hove, Sussex
BN3 2BD

World Federation of Hypnotherapists
The Secretary
Belmont Centre
46 Belmont Road
Ramsgate, Kent
CT11 7QG

Additional addresses for overseas:

For hypnotherapy and counselling

USA
American Association of Professional Hypnotherapists
PO Box 731
McLean, Va. 22101
USA

Australia
Australian Society of Hypnosis
PO Box 366
Glenleg
South Australia 5045

Australian Society for Clinical and Experimental Hypnosis
Royal Melbourne Hospital
Royal Parade
Parkville
Victoria

Canada
Ontario Society for Clinical Hypnosis
170 St George Street, Ste 1001
Toronto
Canada

Index